Reach Out to Horses®
presents

BEYOND
the BARN

EXPLORING THE NEXT GENERATION OF

Horsemanship

Volume 1

ANNA TWINNEY

Beyond the Barn: Exploring the Next Generation of Horsemanship: Volume 1
by Anna Twinney

©2020 by Reach Out to Horses®

Published by

Reach Out to Horses
PO Box 1913
Elizabeth, CO 80107
www.ReachOuttoHorses.com

ISBN: 978-1-7325381-2-2 (print)
ISBN: 978-1-7325381-3-9 (E-book)
LCCN: 2020906667

Copy/Content Editing by John Wilcockson
Book Design by Nick Zelinger, NZGraphics.com
Cover Photo by Tess Helmandollar

First Edition

Printed in the United States of America

Disclaimer:

WORKING WITH HORSES IS A HAZARDOUS ACTIVITY
THAT CAN RESULT IN INJURY AND/OR DEATH.

The authors of this book make no warranties or representations,
and assume no liability concerning the validity of any advice,
opinion, example, demonstration, or recommendation expressed
in this publication.

ALL INDIVIDUALS RELYING UPON THIS MATERIAL DO
SO AT THEIR OWN RISK.

All information shared in this publication is meant to facilitate
health, balance and well-being in an animal. All written materials,
lectures, discussions, questions and answers, references to other
modalities, products, and practitioners are all ways in which
information may be furnished in workshops and consultations.
At no time is this information meant to be a replacement for
traditional medical care, veterinary treatment, or a medical
diagnosis for illness or injury.

Refer to a licensed medical or veterinary practitioner for
medical care and to appropriate professionals for the service you
are seeking.

Contents

PART I

THE MOVEMENT
INTO A METHODOLOGY

1

BEGINNING TO BUILD A BOND THROUGH COMMUNICATION

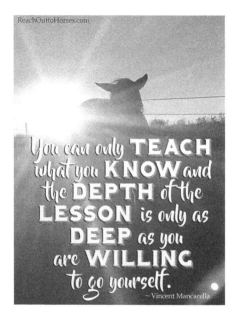

You can only **TEACH** what you **KNOW** and the **DEPTH** of the **LESSON** is only as **DEEP** as you are **WILLING** to go yourself.

~ Vincent Mancarella

Creating a trust-based relationship is the foundation to all interaction and training with your horse. Not only will you achieve better results in the show ring, you will also begin to become one with your horse. Together you will achieve optimum performance while learning about one another and growing as individuals.

Communication with our horses begins upon approach. We communicate non-verbally through our body language, our energy, and simply through our being. It is a known fact that about 90 percent of communication is non-verbal and only 7 percent is spoken. Horses can read us better than we can read ourselves! Upon your approach, they will know how you feel in any given moment, who you are, how you carry yourself, and also your intention. It is important therefore that you are aware of the movements you make and the thoughts you have.

> *"Any excess baggage should be left outside the paddock, stall, or arena, as it is rather unfair to your four-legged friend to take the rap of your day."*

Displacement occurs readily through frustration, which is caused by a lack of understanding and creativity and can easily rear its head at the end of a hard day's work. Knowing and understanding your horse and his communication system will allow for a trust-based partnership to build.

> *"Wild horses communicate in a language called Equus, which is nonverbal and much like signing for the deaf. Each motion, such as a flick of the ear and a swish of the tail, means something."*

It is a language that we are able to interpret and customize through our own body language. Spending time with your horse and observing others in their natural habitat will allow you to experience the language first hand. Try to be present as you notice the movements of the horse and subsequent responses. Every horse has his own personality, character, and role within the herd, and as you familiarize yourself with the group these will become more apparent to you. Behavior will be emphasized during feeding time and rankings are more easily identifiable during this time. Knowing these aspects of your horse will allow you to understand the way horses think and why they respond to certain situations as they do.

Although, for the most part, the language of Equus is non-verbal for preservation purposes, on occasion horses will also become vocal. Domestic horses feel comfortable in their environment to whinny, nicker, snort, squeal, and even snore. Each horse will have his own way of expressing likes and dislikes, fears and concerns, as well as happiness and excitement. Knowing your horse's natural day-to-day behavior will allow you to recognize unusual and abnormal behavior.

A less-spoken-about form of communication is your intuition, also known as your sixth sense, or, as many famous horsemen have coined it, "the feel." This is a form of interspecies communication. We have all experienced times when we are particularly connected to a brother, sister, or close friend, and they have been on our minds for a while. When you finally pick up the phone to call them, both of you mention that you've been thinking of one another—this, believe it or not, is a basic form of telepathy. Your intuition plays a huge part in your relationship with your horse. You may be touched by a feeling or emotion that you know is not your own. You may receive a glance of a vision, hear words, or have a vivid dream. Because it is very personal to everyone, it's hard to describe and teach intuition to others. As you are able to confirm your intuitive hits, you will learn to trust your intuition and this form of communication will become second nature to you.

There are so many facets to encompass when you speak about communication, but I would like to emphasize that horses are social animals. They love to interact, play in groups, or take part in mutual grooming. Find out what your horse likes, what motivates him and be a part of his daily life without an agenda. Instead of thinking what can my horse do for me today, think what it is that you can do for your horse!

2

HORSES AS MASTER TEACHERS

Horses are masters at assessing your body language. They are also able to read your thoughts, intentions, and ultimately the energy surrounding your very being. Even before your arrival at the barn, they can sense how you feel and often reflect it back to you through their being and actions. Horses don't ask much of us, but the most important thing they do ask is that you are present in their presence.

YOU CAN DO THIS BY:

◡ Taking a moment to unwind and ground yourself with deep breathing before you visit your horse.

◡ Being aware of your emotions and making the decision to leave your worries at home. Give yourself permission to enjoy your time together with your horse.

◡ Removing any time pressures. You have the choice to either rush through your experience together or to truly be present and enjoy every moment.

◡ Realizing that strong agendas, focus, and clarity are all good things, but when you refuse to be flexible and these things rule your life you lose sight of what is important.

◡ Being mindful of your thoughts will change the whole relationship with your horse. Notice how much more he connects with you as you share in his silent language. As you quiet your mind, you will create space to capture your horse's whisper through a deeper connection, greater understanding, and more subtle communication. If you find your mind wandering into past or future, simple acknowledge the thought and bring yourself back to the present moment.

From the Horse's Mouth

Riders aren't the only ones with big dreams for themselves and their horses. If horses could talk, they would tell us that they too have hopes, dreams, and desires. Although it's popularly believed that horses are purely interested in survival and reproduction, they may have their own destinies to fulfill and life lessons to live.

It is quite possible that as you meet different horses, you will experience contrasting desires—from horses that prefer freedom in nature with their herds all the way to driven athletes who wish to perform at an Olympic level.

Be open to the idea that you are their voice and are providing them with platforms of opportunity.

Despite the fact that wild horses do not have body workers, coaches, or pedicurists while they roam freely in nature, our domestic counterparts require emotional, mental, and physical support as they venture into show season.

Have a team of experts on hand to support your horse's health and well-being both pre- and post-performance. In addition to veterinary expertise, complementary therapies are essential, with a focus on maximizing health instead of simply treating sickness.

In domestication, inappropriate habits and vices not found in wild horse bands can materialize. In cases such as these, it seems human intervention negatively affects some horse's lifestyles. Assess your horse's living arrangements and make the adjustments needed for him to live as naturally as possible, ensuring optimal health. Although people may shy away from the idea of horses living in open spaces (particularly high-level performance horses), access to a regular source of food and socialization provides them with basic natural needs, prevents inappropriate behavior and optimizes health. This helps create a more positive and powerful performance in the show ring.

3

WHAT YOUR HORSE WANTS YOU TO KNOW

Strive not to be a success, but rather to be of value.
~Albert Einstein

Reach Out to Horses.com

I am privileged to work with people and horses from all over the world. As a Natural Horsewoman and Animal Communicator, I often hear the same requests—not from the humans, but from the horses. Here's what they would like you to do:

1. **Resolve to bring joy and serenity to your interactions with me.** How often have you come to the barn to cry on my shoulder? Sometimes I willingly accept my role as "healer," but occasionally I prefer you to leave your

baggage outside the stall. Being a master of reading energy, I pick up on your emotions and I'm immediately affected by your thoughts. Is how you feel my fault?

2. **Before you enter my stall or paddock, find out what is happening in my world.** In an ideal world you would spend all of your time with me, but your life often gets in the way. Because you don't see me all the time, you cannot always be aware of my experiences throughout the day. Maybe I woke up on the wrong side of the stall, or my companion passed away or was sold. Perhaps something spooked me or I feel under the weather.

3. **Consider my wishes.** How would you feel if you couldn't follow your dreams or your destiny? Trapped? Lost? Stuck? Maybe you would act out or fall into depression. I also have a personal path, a destiny to follow. My dreams may not fit perfectly with yours but, as you would with any partner, try to understand and respect my wishes too.

4. **Let me show you how to be in the now.** So often you fill any silence with noise. It's time to put the cell phone down, stop the constant chatter with your riding buddy, and instead be present, connect with me and with nature.

5. **Be flexible with your plan.** Many times, you have goals and lesson plans in mind when "training" me; this doesn't always allow me to have a voice. Listen to your heart, your intuition, and, above all, me. Maybe today you'll sit with me as I eat and experience the magic of togetherness.

6. **You are family and your home is my home.** Unlike your canine companions, my fellow horses are often sold when they no longer fit in, are discarded when the show is over, or are let go at the first sign of pain or lameness. Remember, we trust you. Retire us with ease, considering what makes us happy. Repay me with the same unconditional kindness and devotion I gave you for my entire life.

7. **Grant me dignity in death.** You may feel it's "time for me to cross over." Before you make any decisions, connect with me and listen to my last wishes. I'm willing to share where, when, and how I wish to cross over, who I wish to have present, and the time I need to visit, say "goodbye," and share my messages. Remember to give me this final chance.

4

FOR THE GOOD OF YOUR HORSE

INTUITION IS NOT A *lightbulb* WAITING TO BE SWITCHED ON INSIDE THE MIND. IT IS A *small ember* READY TO BE *ignited* BY SIMPLY *trusting* IN ONE'S SELF.

REACHOUTTOHORSES.COM

1. Horses speak in a silent language unique to them, namely the language of Equus. Through intricate gestures in body language, they communicate within their herd and often the whisper can be captured in their eye. The energetic connection and interspecies communication cannot necessarily be seen, but it can be felt and received by us. ***Learn to listen to your horse's whisper.***

2. As a social species, horses live naturally in herds to feel safe. For the herd to run smoothly, the horses all have specific roles, be it to learn, grow up, play, nurture,

protect, reproduce, or guide. Friendships and bonds form with other animals, but there is no real substitute for their own kind. *Consider your horse's need to bond and connect with other horses.*

3. It's not about the destination; it's about the journey. Enjoy the process of learning about your horse's needs. Embrace every opportunity to watch, listen, and learn. Your horse wants you to be an active participant in his everyday care from exercise, hoof care, nutrition, dentistry, and healthcare, through to a personal-exercise program. *For the good of your horse, "be present."*

4. Like us, horses express themselves through their actions. Actions often speak louder than words. In order to be understood and heard, many horses will show their physical limitations, fears, concerns, and pain through behavioral challenges. When the whisper is not caught, these actions appear to us through evasion, resistance, anxiety, anger, and "acting out." *Realize when your horse is not himself, he may be in pain.*

5. As humans, we are able to release our emotions through tears. We are able to cry to the extent of sobbing. We can lean on others to help us through the hard times and they are willing to take on our heartache and pain. Horses can also shed tears, but are unable to cry to the same extent that we can. When you feel yourself about to cry and you know the tears are not your own, let the tears flow, for you can become a conduit. *You may experience releasing tears for the horses.*

6. Horses can pick up our thoughts. Our riding posture and imbalances can be reflected in our horse's movements. Our emotional challenges can be reflected in our horse's behavior. Our physical issues can be taken on and manifested by our horses. *Horses are our mirrors; be sure to look at the reflection.*

7. There is no such thing as a coincidence. Each animal crosses our path for a reason and your horse is no exception! Open your mind and listen to your heart to discover the lessons brought to you by your horse—the life lessons. *The horse remains your best teacher.*

5

A Personal Program vs. a Cookie-Cutter System

Seek first to Understand

then

to be Understood

Steven Covey

REACHOUTTOHORSES.COM

---

*"Creating a trust-based relationship is the foundation
to all interaction and training with your horse.
That is why the foundation of any training program
I create is communication."*

Someone once told me, while I was training an orphan foal to trailer load, that the horse is a prey animal, so "you have to use fear to get the horse to do what you need."

I had no interest in learning anything about this youngster's background, the gentle training he had received during the week, or the fact that he was leaving foals behind with whom he had a strong bond since his rescue.

His thought was simply: "Get it done."

Up until this very moment, our foal had been listened to, all his tries were acknowledged, and our relationship had been built on trust. Each lesson had been short, building one upon the other, for him to find his true potential.

We were not about to destroy all we had worked for, or break our word to never hurt him and prove to him we were untrustworthy. Our time together had been about earning his trust since he was taken from his mother early and discarded at the feedlot. It was a crucial time to avoid undue pressure, to show him that we could be trusted, and to recognize his concerns about entering the unknown trailer.

My intention was pure, my attention was in the moment, and he was given reassurance that he would be met by a herd of horses out in pasture. It was a matter of staying in one's truth and not being blindsided by the growing audience that was coming to help and offer its advice.

"Once you give your horse a voice, be ready and willing to hear what he has to say."

The statements made by our onlookers are pretty typical training strategies that are prevalent in the horse industry. The idea is that if you make it more uncomfortable for the horse to do what you don't want and comfortable to do what you do want, you'll get the results desired with compliance and control paving the way.

Although effective on occasion, and arguably necessary in an emergency, it doesn't allow the horse a voice and doesn't give the horse a chance to decide to work with you. Instead, it treats every horse the same. It treats them like "a horse," but not as an individual or, indeed, a partner. You certainly can use this method, but you don't have to. You have a choice . . . a better choice.

As I meet people from all over the world, of all different philosophies, disciplines, and cultures, I often come up against one common request: the desire to find the "one-size-fits-all" answer and step-by-step program. They long to follow the steps that, when finished, will give them the compliant horse that will do whatever is asked, whenever it's asked.

I can certainly understand the desire. If you could learn a simple, quick, and effective method that worked on all horses, there would be no need for thought, creativity, troubleshooting, or any kind of real expertise. You'd simply walk your horse through the steps and your "push button" companion would be ready to go.

However, real partnership includes mutual cooperation and responsibility, and in order to achieve that, both parties need to be active participants. Just like humans, horses are individuals. If you train all horses the same way, at best you get an equine robot, a mindless creature doing what it was trained to do. You will never have a willing companion or a relationship built on trust.

At worst, you will create a whole list of undesirable behaviors that will need fixing at a later date—provided, of course, you haven't suffered any serious injuries from a poorly trained horse. And what happens if your training doesn't work? Then what do you do? You have no other tools you can use and this is when the temptation to use violence to gain submission is at its highest.

In short, all your training is work you are doing *to the horse, not with the horse.*

If you are looking for total compliance, then I would strongly suggest you buy a motorcycle, ATV, or some other form of motorized transportation. It is sure to do whatever you ask.

But my guess is that isn't what you want. You have come to the horse for the relationship you can only have with an equine partner. You seek an individual, a competition partner, a riding companion, a friend.

If that is what you seek, then you must have a training program created in trust-based methodologies that are designed to work with the unique make-up of your horse. You must take into consideration your horse as an individual. Be excited and explore your equine partner's story. Let him share with you who he truly is and how best to communicate and work together—it's a journey of discovery!

"There's no such thing as a bad horse, only bad training."

Listen, learn, and love the discovery of how and why all of these areas make-up your horse: *personality, temperament, learning style, sex, breed, discipline, character, environment, history, memories, and more.*

That is why the foundation of any training program I create is communication. By communication I don't mean simple body language or physical cues. The horse's language is subtle and simple within its comprehensive complexity and goes far beyond just the physical.

I use all the tools at my disposal to silently "speak" to the horse, discover who he is, what makes him tick, and develop a customized program just for him. Through this methodology, I am able to prove to the horse that I am worthy of this trust, and the horse is given the time and space to develop that trust at his pace. The training methodologies adopted are based on each individual horse; by understanding and working with your horse, you are setting him up for success and a life of real trust-based partnership.

Imagine being able to learn a horse's unspoken language, rather than just teaching him your training style.

You might be thinking that this strategy would take far too long to be practical for a training program. You would be mistaken; as with any tool, it is dependent on the hands that wield it. When used properly, these methodologies are just as fast as (if not faster than) any other method and have very little chance of creating behavioral problems. They are safe and effective and give a voice to the voiceless. However, not everyone is ready and willing to hear what their horses have to say.

WARNING:
Once you give your horse a voice, be ready and willing
to hear what he has to say.

Remember, there's no such thing as a bad horse; only bad training, or rather, inappropriate training. Instead of believing there is only one way, or your horse is "acting out," realize he is attempting to tell you something. It may be that he's in pain, experiencing a misunderstanding, or there's a lack of clarity within the communication. After all, sometimes it is smooth and other times we have to work on relationships.

It is not about comparing how other horses are performing, it is only about you and your horse. The more you work with your horse as the individual he or she is and develop a training program that fits, and the more you learn to learn to truly communicate with your horse, the better results you will achieve.

6

YOUR HORSE IS IN YOUR LIFE FOR A REASON

There is no such thing as coincidence.
Our horses are in our lives for a reason.

ReachOut[of]orses.com   Anna & Excalibur

Some may tell you to sell a particular horse to find the "right fit" for him or her. But what if this horse is in your life for a specific reason, a reason you have always known was there? Once you realize there is no such thing as a coincidence, you can begin to look more deeply at the messages and life lessons your partnership with your horse can reveal.

- Begin to examine how you feel around your horse. What emotions does he or she evoke within you? *If you are being emotionally challenged, how can you place a positive spin on the situation?*

- What effect does your horse have on your horsemanship skills? *You may be receiving gentle coaching from an equine schoolmaster or, conversely, being asked to stretch your limits.*

- Consider if you are on the right path. *Horses ask us to walk the path of authenticity, reflecting our truth through their responses and mannerisms.*

Undoubtedly, horses are our teachers. The lessons are often clear, but other times they can be deeper and one has to look through the veil to uncover the message. When we take the time to reflect upon our relationship and check in by asking ourselves, "What am I here to learn?" the answer shows itself to us. It's time to tune into our intuition, think outside the box, realize there is a larger purpose, and thank our horses for their clarity and commitment to the cause.

7

LEARNING TO SPEAK YOUR HORSE'S LANGUAGE

A Guide to Better Communication

THERE ARE TWO WAYS TO SPREAD LIGHT

BE THE CANDLE

OR THE MIRROR THAT REFLECTS

ReachOuttoHorses.com

When clarity and compassion replace fear and frustration,
you will achieve the bond you've been looking for.

When we work with our horses, it is not uncommon for us to consider what is best for them and our partnership from our own human perspective. But if we take a moment to look through our horses' eyes we will gain a new and intimate perspective. We will come to understand a little more about the way they see the world and gain a better appreciation for the contributions and sacrifices they make for us.

Through communication, connection, and collaboration, we can transform our less-than-effective leadership and eliminate the dreaded feeling of being out of control, for both the horse and the human.

Here's how to make it happen:

- **Begin to learn and speak their language:** Recognize horses' minute gestures—this is how they communicate. These gestures are nearly undetectable and require a keen eye to be noticed. The slightest of movements—a subtle shift in weight distribution, a look in his eye, the direction of his ears—are all movements that open up and create a dialogue.

- **Familiarize yourself with their culture:** Horses work together in a herd hierarchy, where each individual has a role and a purpose. They come together for a mutual purpose and gain strength in their community. There are certain rituals that hold strong, including the waterhole, sharing space, and eating rituals. With knowledge and recognition of their desire for a natural habitat and lifestyle, we gain a greater understanding of their sacrifices and needs.

- **Ground yourself:** Let the stresses of your day dissolve. Remember to breathe! Take some deep breaths. Allow the flow of your breathing to release any tension you might be carrying. A walk within nature will allow your worries and sorrows to disappear as Mother Earth replenishes and returns you to balance. Or envision love flowing through your heart into your hands and your very being. Then bring that energy and intention to the horses.

- **Hold a positive attitude:** You must put your fears and concerns aside to be able to achieve your goal.

- **Achieve your goals organically:** This happens naturally as your partnership evolves. Keep your intentions pure; never fixate on achieving your goal at any cost.

- **Celebrate his every success:** Praise your horse in the manner he understands and embraces. He may appreciate a light touch, a rub on the neck or shoulder or a moment's break. He will realize your every thought and intention behind it. Remember to breathe and smile as you acknowledge his tries and recognize all attempts to do his best on that day. A soft voice, a moment's recognition, and shared joy go a long way.

- **Encourage your horse's individual character:** Let his personality develop and shine through. When you learn to recognize his nuances, you can read his intentions through his eyes before he makes a move.

- **Be driven by exploration, expansion, creativity, and collaboration:** When you are no longer task-oriented, dominance takes a back seat. Through interactive engagement in your initial daily activities and responsibilities, your horse is given both a voice and a choice.

- **Respond with kindness:** No matter how young or old, unhandled or over handled, innocent or wise, no horse needs to be treated with callous convenience—as simply . . . a horse.

- **Take note of his learning style:** Figure out the length of lesson he appreciates. They should be on his time, not yours, so he is able to process and retain the information provided.

- **Keep variety in your sessions:** Use your creativity and adjust the time you may need to repeat aspects of your repertoire for mutual understanding. Working in reciprocity will always yield better results than imposing your will onto him.

When we consider things from their perspective, their resistance isn't so perplexing. For example, if your horse is responding negatively to his halter, remember that it is likely he was taught by his elders to protect his head from all handling. As prey animals, it is natural for them to be driven by fear; to hide, disassociate, do their best to run away, and, if necessary, fight for their lives.

It is without a doubt the more difficult journey, the road less travelled. It can be frustratingly more challenging than simply demanding that horses meet us where we are, or forcing them to abide by a systemized approach. If we expect them to try and bring their best to us, then we must do the same for them. We must replace force, dominance, and compliance with compassion, communication, and collaboration.

PART II

THE EXPLORATION AND EVOLUTION OF THE NEXT GENERATION OF HORSEMANSHIP

8

TO TREAT OR NOT TO TREAT

ReachOuttoHorses.com

Um ... This thing is empty. I brought it to you ... You're Welcome!

"The way to a man's heart is through his stomach." We've all heard that saying. I would love to concur but unfortunately I don't cook, so where does that leave me? Happily married, exploring other ways to express my affection, I'm pleased to say.

As human beings, it's only natural for us to want to nurture the ones we love, especially our animal companions. All too often though, in the case of our horses, we humanize their needs and sometimes can do more harm than good without even realizing it. What most people don't realize is that horses are not trophy animals. You cannot bribe a horse into liking you or doing what you want them to do.

They don't see food as that kind of reward. As herbivores, grass is always freely available and it never tries to run away from them. In a horse's mind, for example, if you have food in your pocket and you hand-feed it to him, he is expecting that food to be there all the time!

So, you can see how hand feeding can cause some serious problems. Who hasn't had a horse search (a.k.a., "mug") them for food only to have the horse look more firmly when they come up empty? And fun can quickly turn dangerous when he starts biting your clothing or even worse, you! If you are not careful, your horse will begin to see you as a food dispenser and when the dispenser is empty, it can leave you with one angry horse.

By not handfeeding, on the other hand, you also avoid the issue of boundary breaking and disrespect when your horse enters your personal space and thereby exposes you to possible injuries caused by headbutting, striking, or running over the top of you. Instead, you create a mutual relationship whereby you both respect one another's personal space and enter only upon invitation.

"Create a mutual relationship whereby you both respect one another's personal space and enter only upon invitation."

These same treats are not only given as a sign of our affection but also as a reward for your horse's performance. Many owners give their horses carrots, mints, or cookies as a sign of appreciation for gaining a "clear round" showjumping, in appreciation for winning a competition, or merely to show appreciation for "behaving" well during a trail ride. What could possibly be wrong with that, right? Well, if you take a moment to view the world through your horse's eyes, you'll see that your horse may not quite think of that treat the same way you do.

You are chomping away at your hay, relaxing as you enjoy the sunrise out of your window. Your person arrives in her best attire, her hair pulled back and placed in a bun with a net to keep it tidy. You notice her beautifully clean jodhpurs and see your image reflected in her shiny black boots. You read her energy and feel the excitement in her movements as your memory bank is jogged. The last time she arrived in your stall looking like this, you left your stable and went on an outing! You now realize why you were groomed particularly well earlier this morning and all the time you had thought it was "massage day." Your mane has been braided to show off your magnificent neck and your whole body smells like spring blossom. Ahhhh, yes, now the excitement builds in you. It's show time!

A short time later, you arrive at the show ring. Looking around, everything is new to you: the grandstands, the sounds coming over the microphone, children running around, dogs barking, strange colors everywhere, and a whole range of horses who begin to fill your mind with their own personal stories. In fact, some horses are being lunged in circles to calm them down while others are bucking out of pure delight. You are not sure how you feel exactly, but you try to take in the whole environment as your person mounts and promptly gives you cues to follow. There is no time to get acclimatized to this new place.

You feel somewhat overwhelmed and yet you want to do your best. You feel the desire to please your person and now you try to focus. You are familiar with the warm-up ring and instantly know that it's nearing your time to perform. Your name is called and proudly you enter the show ring. You are at one with your person, you feel their every movement and their every request, and you don't hesitate to oblige. Diligently you pace yourself, feeling for all cues and deciphering them every step of the way. You feel as though you are on top form, working every muscle efficiently, and truly giving your all.

You know the course is over as you feel a pat on the neck and then you leave the show ring to be cooled down, untacked, watered, and taken home. You ask yourself, "Where are the carrots, the apples and all the wonderful tasty treats I usually get?" You don't understand that this time just wasn't good enough, this time you knocked down a pole.

Most of us know what it feels like to be reprimanded for not accomplishing our best. There have been times in our lives when we have been punished or scolded for not getting the results or marks that had been expected and yet we have given our all. Maybe no one knew how much effort went in behind the scenes, but it's often these scenes that we remember and form part of who we are today. We all respond in different ways. Maybe you withdrew, maybe you lashed out, maybe you played hooky, or maybe it created the drive that you needed!

"If you take a moment to view the world through your horse's eyes, you'll see that your horse may not quite think of that treat the same way you do."

Every horse will have its individual response too. They don't understand why the food didn't appear on this occasion. Some horses will become extraordinarily aggressive or impatient and paw at the ground in anticipation, while others will sulk or withdraw. If you are lucky, your horse will forgive you. To them it doesn't make sense that the treats didn't appear; they associate the experience with the usual treat.

Now is the time to make a change. Reward your horse every time they try! You will encourage them to want to perform, and they will become motivated and engage in the activity. You both deserve it!

We all enjoy the odd sugar rush! So, if you follow these simple tips, you'll be able to safely give your horse the treats he loves and so well deserves.

- Always give the treats from a container such as a bucket or in your horse's feed bin, never out of the hand.

- Don't be afraid to show your horse how much you appreciate him. Just make sure you give the appreciation in the "right" way.

- Timing is crucial when giving treats as a reward. Optimum timing is three- to eight-tenths of a second from the behavior. Anything more than that and your horse may not make the connection between the behavior and the treat.

- Treats can calm horses and create a place of safety and comfort.

Knowing how to use food as a reward and when to replace it or intermingle it with praise, release of pressure, or rest is the key.

Learn how to properly use the treats and you'll be able to treat your horse in a way that makes you the leader of the herd of two and not the pushover treat dispenser.

It's All in the Timing

When teaching a horse, timing is everything. Horses are associative thinkers, so they link reprimands and rewards with the preceding action. Although they are able to link an action to a response within three seconds, the optimum timing is from three- to eight-tenths of a second. In other words, you should ideally respond within a window of one second!

This means that if your horse accepts a stimulus, such as a plastic bag, in a calm manner, it is time for you to remove the stimulus. Calm means that he is standing still, relaxing his head, or licking and chewing. He may also display other signs that communicate he is relaxed.

If you wait too long, however, and this causes distress to your horse, he may become anxious. He could display this by pawing, moving around, raising his head high, or lifting his tail in preparation to run. If you remove the stimulus at this time, you are, in fact, rewarding the undesirable behavior! Stay present and be aware of what exactly you are looking for in your horse.

9

BITING THEIR WAY INTO YOUR HEART?

THE MORE REFLECTIVE YOU ARE, THE **MORE** EFFECTIVE YOU ARE.

REACHOUTTOHORSES.COM

"Just like humans, horses have normal stages of development they must go through in order to become well-adjusted adults."

"Before you enforce strong personal boundaries, it is always good to consider what your horse is doing and if his actions truly need changing."

"Learning to read your horse and understand what he is saying is imperative for any horse owner."

For a short period during his formative years as a young colt, my mustang, Excalibur, decided it was time to be mouthy. He was at the prime age to explore foreign objects with his lips and muzzled everything he could find. He enjoyed learning about all types of textures, tastes, and smells—which ultimately is a good thing. During this process, however, he decided to try his luck with me. Not his best decision to date, and what began as exploration ventured into a "game" as he amused himself with nipping me when my back was turned. I tried numerous times to reprimand him but that was useless; just part of the game to him. Finally, I was able to increase the stakes to create a very clear boundary and put an end to this playtime exercise, at least for the day.

"Once you know your horse's baseline, or usual behavior patterns, you will recognize abnormal or unusual behavior."

"If we perceive an obstacle as difficult or impossible to overcome, for example, we may become fearful and, at times, mask this fear with aggression."

"Support instead of conflict is always a better solution."

I'm sure, if you've raised a horse from colt or filly to adulthood, you can understand exactly what I was going through. Just like humans, horses have normal stages of development they must go through in order to become well-adjusted adults. Unlike humans, though, horses' jaws are very powerful, and it

can be quite intimidating to watch an open mouth coming toward you or suddenly find yourself in between a set of teeth! In order to explore effective solutions to this
     occasionally painful endeavor, you must become very adept at interpreting and understanding your horse's behavior. A great place to start with a biting challenge (or any challenge for that matter) is to ask yourself these questions:

When did this behavior begin?
What triggered this behavior today?
How does this behavior show itself?
Where does it happen?
Who is involved?
Why is this behavior happening?
When do we need to have it solved by?

Once you've answered these questions to the best of your ability, it is time to determine the most important factor in behavioral change: Does this behavior really need to be changed? Now, obviously, if your horse is doing something that could potentially be dangerous to him or to you, the answer would be a resounding "yes!"

But before you enforce strong personal boundaries it is always good to consider what your horse is doing and if his actions truly need changing. For example, some horses may lick your hands or arms seeking additional salt in their diets or simply because they enjoy the taste of your leftovers. After all, they love sweet and salty tastes. So, you may go through a lot of trouble to change behavior when the real answer was to give them more salt, or to just let them enjoy the taste!

Regardless of the behavior or the decision to change it, the more information you have about the behavior, the better equipped you'll be to solve the problem. Knowing why your horse is doing what he is doing is a crucial step in the process. So, here are some common reasons to consider when it comes to your horse's behavior and how to approach changing and shaping the behavior when you need to do so.

Signs of Affection

By their very nature, horses are affectionate and explore people with their muzzles. They like to touch, feel, and smell different body parts. Often, when horses become very comfortable, they engage in what is called "mutual grooming," seeking different locations to massage you with their upper lip! These can all be signs of affection and you need to decide whether or not you want to invite this behavior into your life. If you decide to embrace these offerings, ensure that everyone is on the same page, so that your horse doesn't get encouraged by one person while being reprimanded by another for the exact same gesture. Consistency is the key here!

For safety reasons, you may keep certain horses out of your personal range, whereas others are invited into close proximity. It is acceptable to encourage some to touch you with their lips and yet prohibit the opening of their mouth or placement of teeth. These are your decisions—for you know your horse best, or at least you should—and what is comfortable and acceptable to you!

Signs of Discomfort

Learning to read your horse and understand what he is saying is imperative for any horse owner. Horses can show signs of mental, emotional, and physical discomfort and it is important that you are able to identify what your horse is trying to say. Horses in pain may try to bite while tacking up. Often known as "cinchy horses," they attempt to tell you about backache, discomfort, sensitivity, saddle fitting, and anxiety just to name a few. Always consult a vet if you believe there is a physical reason for their behavior.

Horses have lifelong memories and it takes patience, trust, and compassion to overcome previously uncomfortable experiences. They may anticipate an action triggered from their past.

During the saddling of young horses, I've experienced their attempt to bite at the girth, the stirrup irons, or my arm. This behavior may be a natural response, exploring the situation. On the other hand, it may also be an expression of concern or of an overzealous nature. This same behavior may disappear in just a few days as their confidence builds (known as extinction).

Once you know your horse's baseline, or usual behavior patterns, you will recognize abnormal or unusual behavior. If your horse never bites and suddenly displays aggressive tendencies during a new or unusual request, consider that he may be confused or you might have overloaded him mentally or emotionally with your request. Ask yourself how many signs of anxiety you missed prior and if schooling him would be appropriate due to your oversight.

Signs of Aggression

There are many reasons why horses become aggressive; what I believe to be certain is that *"NO horse is born bad!"*

Characteristics and behavior can be based on bloodlines, environment, and influence. Many times, our horses are victims of our innocence and ignorance and, as such, can become defensive, often appearing aggressive.

The cause behind aggression is always fear. The acronym of F.E.A.R.—" false evidence appearing real"—applies to horses just as much as it does to humans. This isn't to say that the feelings of fear aren't real, but instead that we are experiencing those feelings based on the reality we've created through our perceptions. If we perceive an obstacle as difficult or impossible to overcome, for example, we may become fearful and, at times, mask this fear with aggression.

Everyone knows the cliché of the child who yells, "Leave me alone!" or "I don't want to!" because he is afraid of something and doesn't want to face it. The same is true for your horse. If you can unravel the cause of this behavior, get to the core fear your horse is experiencing, you will solve the aggressive tendencies without having to get aggressive yourself.

Support instead of conflict is always a better solution.

Remember, your horse is just trying to tell you something and it's not his fault. With patience and understanding, this too shall pass.

Signs of Play

Many times, horses can simply think they are being playful. Their intention is not to harm in any way. They just want to have some fun and don't understand that what they are doing can be harmful or dangerous. In Excalibur's case above, for example, it is not unusual for testosterone-driven colts to be confident and challenging at this age. In addition, he had been stall-bound for several weeks, due to discomfort, and was carrying a lot of pent-up energy.

Insufficient exercise during the day creates a buildup of energy just waiting to be released and can sometimes show itself as destructive. Feed schedule is another consideration; it is important to ensure the quantity of feed matches the workload. There are so many possibilities that it is important to stay alert to the fact that your horse, like an overzealous older sibling, just might be excited, not realizing that he could do harm in his enthusiastic desire to play.

Your Toolbox!

Once you have explored the answers to your questions and you know there is no physical discomfort behind your horse's actions, you are ready to address this undesirable behavior. Your methods need to be mixed and matched to suit your horse's needs at the time, as well as suiting your own personal comfort level. No one horse is the same and hence your "tools" are exactly that.

They are not "fix it all" solutions; they are tools for you to use and explore as you make your way to shaping and changing your horse's behavior.

As with all horsemanship, the quantity of pressure, its release, timing, and reward are all keys to your success.

Work vs. Rest

This is probably my favorite method for addressing the serious biter. I usually utilize a round pen in these situations. Having entered the round pen, I begin my session by "reaching out" to my horse to gain insights into his personality while building mutual trust, understanding, and respect. Once we have achieved the basic contract, we create scenarios conducive to intrinsic learning.

"Always praise your horse for any attempt to be calm and acknowledge the efforts in ways perceived as praise (rest, rubs, release of pressure)."

"Sometimes the best thing to do is nothing."

"Always remember that some of these lessons can be avoided with correct management— prevention is better than cure!"

"What makes good horsemen or women is the confidence and ability to determine what is appropriate for them and their horse."

For example, positioned in the center of the round pen, a place of comfort and rest, I clip a short lead rope (approximately ten inches in length) onto my horse's halter. You can use an old lead line that has been cut to the desired length. This enables me to lead my horse as normal. If and when my "student" becomes invasive or attempts to bite, there are consequences for his actions; he gets put to work, this time running around the perimeter of the round pen.

After certain gestures, he is invited to join me in the center of the round pen and within a short period of time, he learns to behave in the correct manner so he may stay close. After all, he doesn't want to be banished from the herd and neither does he want to keep exercising. Lavished with support and comfort in the center of the pen, he is encouraged to be respectful where life is easier and restful.

Comfort vs. Discomfort

If you are one of the many people who do not have access to a round pen or arena, you may wish to utilize the concept of comfort vs. discomfort. The principles are identical in nature to work vs. rest. If your horse misbehaves—that is, attempts to bite you—back him up!

Horses don't back up in nature over any distance. You are, in fact, not only putting your horse to work, but by moving backward he is giving you control of his feet. Also, by asking him to back into his blind spot directly behind him, you are building trust, but at the same time, by creating space between you and him, you are, in effect, banishing him from your herd of two.

It has multiple lessons and is very effective. Remember this shouldn't be an "all negative" lesson; always praise your horse for any attempt to be calm and acknowledge the efforts in ways perceived as praise (rest, rubs, release of pressure).

Distraction

You may have heard that horses only concentrate on one sensation and stimulus at a time. Although I question this statement, I have found distraction to be an occasionally effective tool. An example of this would be a "playful" individual trying to engage you in a round of nipping just to witness your reaction. As your horse prepares to bite you, distract him. One suggestion may be to tap your horse on his nearside front fetlock with your foot. Notice I said "tap" not "kick." This distracts him from his original thought pattern. It is believed that a horse will not associate this action with you, but don't be fooled by this every time. Horses learn right and wrong very quickly!

Extinction

Sometimes the best thing to do is nothing. Like a child trying to get attention, if you simply ignore the behavior, it will die out naturally. This can be very effective when training young or immature horses. You choose your topics to address with your tools and let the others just disappear!

Bumping

Allow your horse to naturally bump into your elbow or other body parts, such as your shoulder, hip, or backside. There is no hitting or smacking involved, no chasing your horse down or preempting his actions. It's a matter of staying firmly in position and in a timely fashion, allowing him to bump his nose. It is always about timing! The horse causes his own discomfort and soon realizes that biting is not as much fun as he thought it would be.

As you can see, there are a lot of tools you can use when solving your biting problem. But the most important tool you have is your own creativity. Horses are living, breathing creatures, not computers or mechanical objects. You can't just push a button or apply a technique and expect it to work every time.

If one approach doesn't work then try another. Be patient, always pay attention, and don't be afraid to try something just because someone else told you it wouldn't work. And always remember that some of these lessons can be avoided with correct management—prevention is better than cure!

The last thing to keep in mind is that the answer always comes down to you. What will ultimately determine the work to be done is your common sense and comfort level. Don't look to a formula or someone else's word to decide what is acceptable and what isn't. What makes good horsemen or women is the confidence and ability to determine what is appropriate for them and their horse. So, stay safe, learn what makes your horse tick, and with time and training you can solve that biting challenge and have a very well-behaved horse.

10

BITING UNCOVERED

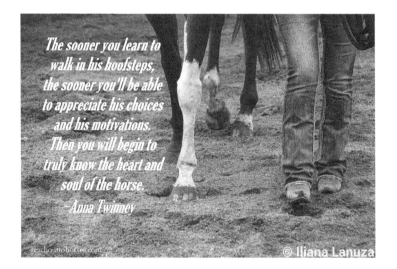

The sooner you learn to walk in his hoofsteps, the sooner you'll be able to appreciate his choices and his motivations. Then you will begin to truly know the heart and soul of the horse.
~Anna Twinney

reachouttohorses.com © Iliana Lanuza

When training a bad habit or behavior out of a horse, consistency from everyone and at all times *is crucial.*

Many conclusions had been drawn by those who knew him, but I knew that listening to Hermano himself would give us the answers and direction we needed to rectify the current situation.

Biting is one of those problems that all horse lovers come across at one time or another. It can be a very frustrating challenge to tackle, not to mention a dangerous one. A biting horse can be a real concern for not only the owner but also the barn staff, grooms, other boarders, and pretty much anyone who comes in contact with the horse. Hermano was one of those horses. He was majestic, powerful, determined, masculine, and a biter.

I met him on a trip to the East Coast, where I went to help with a number of my clients' equine problems. Hermano was known to attack people and kick innocent individuals who were not paying attention to him while on his aisle. He certainly didn't disappoint during our first meeting. His calm demeanor suddenly turned ferocious with his ears pinned back, and my swift, instinctive move away saved me from losing a chunk of my shoulder. It was very clear that, for the safety of everyone in the barn, this was not acceptable behavior.

I asked about Hermano's biting history and it appeared that most of the behavior occurred either in or close to Hermano's stall, when he would lunge at passersby, or while on the crossties in the barn aisle. As I was listening, Hermano reached toward me with his neck, persistently smelling my clothing and seeking what appeared to be snacks. Without hesitation I announced:

"Someone is hand-feeding him treats and this needs to stop as he can't handle the disappointment if he doesn't get a treat. He sees humans as treat dispensers and when they don't deliver, he gets very upset."

"It's not just me," my client announced, in her defense. "It would be difficult to stop everyone from treating him here in the barn." I turned to Julie, the barn manager, and asked whether it would be possible to enforce this request and she immediately supported the idea. When training a bad habit or behavior out of a horse, consistency from everyone and at all times, is crucial and Julie understood that.

Sometimes issues like biting can be directly attributed to unnoticed physical pain or discomfort. That is one of the first things I look for in an uncooperative horse.

The next step was to see Hermano in action. He was led out of his stall and placed on the cross ties in the barn aisle. Although not an advocate of this particular means of tying, it was the norm at this barn and we wanted to reenact the situation as closely to the real thing as possible. Again, Hermano didn't disappoint. Up came his adrenaline as he grew by several inches in height.

While posturing his neck, he began to bite at my client as she touched his sides, imitating grooming and tacking up. Warning all those around him, Hermano raised and danced on his hind feet while swishing his tail in disgust. I could feel the energy bubble he built around himself keeping everyone at bay and instantly demanding respect. He had defined his domain.

Now came the hard part: figuring out the cause of this behavior, not only to establish the depth and degree of his aggression, but also to create a clear plan of action for everyone to follow.

First, I wondered how much of this was Hermano's true nature? Did his bloodline, herd hierarchy, previous history, self-defense affect him, or was this behavior purely based on inappropriate manners? Those who knew him had drawn many conclusions, but I knew that listening to Hermano himself would give us the answers and direction we needed to rectify the current situation.

The Round Pen Experience

I realized the risk I would be taking of a possible attack as I ventured outside to the round pen where Hermano and I would engage in a conversation at liberty. Here, I began to "reach out" to Hermano, a method I use to determine the characters and personalities of horses as equal partners. I asked Hermano to do multiple tasks whereby he would come to understand that I spoke his language, the "language of Equus."

Through gestures and movements, Hermano was asked to explore his path in all three gaits rhythmically, including exploring his flight path, as well as listen to my other requests. I would listen to his responses and needs along the way. I then raised the bar by including turns, gait changes, "whispers" (a.k.a., light gestures) and "shouts" (stronger uses of body language), all the while Hermano remained respectful, responsive, and rhythmic.

Biting, kicking, and being unruly wasn't his natural way. This was his true nature, for he was at liberty and, as such, we were automatically presented with a situation based on equal terms. No whips, or paraphernalia were involved, just him and me. I had my character read and he knew who I was, creating a base on which to work together.

Vulnerable Areas for All

Sometimes issues like biting can be directly attributed to unnoticed physical pain or discomfort. That is one of the first things I look for in an uncooperative horse. But for Hermano this was definitely not the case. Prior vet examinations had all shown that he was not suffering from any pain or discomfort in his body to reflect his behavior pattern. Furthermore, under direct supervision from a very thorough barn manager, he was on a balanced nutritional plan and regularly received massage and other complementary therapies.

Next, several staff members joined me in the round pen as we lavished Hermano with attention. Rubbing our hands all over his body, we massaged him while exploring sensitive areas, hot spots, and pleasure zones. When entering his vulnerable areas (such as around his rib cage and throat, and underneath his belly) we reassured Hermano that he could take our actions on face value and acknowledged his ability to stand still and quiet. We approached him from all angles, all speeds, and included multiple people to induce possible anger or aggression. This didn't seem to trigger anything. So, I could then rule out human interaction and crowding as the cause to his behavior.

Saddle Up

The next step: the saddle. My client mentioned that this may exacerbate the biting, for up until now I had not been able to trigger any of his biting behavior. The English saddle was brought to the center of the round pen where a number of us stayed to tack up Hermano. It was the first time he experienced this many people around him and yet he remained focused and respectful. As we purposefully took our time, included slight intentional "mishaps," and tacked him up multiple times, there was not one single bite. The saddle itself had been fitted perfectly and checked regularly to ensure it fitted him correctly. Tacking up and saddle-fitting was not the cause.

Close Quarters

Finally, it was suggested that Hermano may be claustrophobic and that could be the underlying cause to all his problems. Maybe he just didn't approve of people being so close to him in tight quarters and that the round pen was too open to allow this particular behavior to show itself.

I suggested we take Hermano to another part of the barn and not his "home," an area that he was not necessarily accustomed to and yet one that would provide us with similar insights. Hermano was taken to a stall used for tacking up with the identical layout of his barn aisle. Within this stall he was prepared, once again, for grooming and tacking up. Somewhat distracted, he was intrigued by the smells of the resident stallions and yet remained calm throughout. Accepting all that we brought to the lesson, Hermano showed no signs of claustrophobia or distress.

Conclusion

With many possible causes tested and debunked, I suggested my client build the following procedures into her training program:

* Discontinue hand feeding

* Turnout prior to my client's arrival to eliminate any excess energy levels

* Use of the Dually pressure halter for schooling purposes

* Mutual respect and understanding of Hermano's space

Each scenario we tried was specifically created to explore different possibilities, aspects, and causes to the behavior. Through these exercises, we broke down, layer by layer, to uncover the root cause of his behavior.

We were dealing with a conditioned response, one that could be reconditioned with the help and cooperation of the same people who had unintentionally created the problem in the first place.

Hermano had clearly learned to protect his stall and barn aisle and, in my opinion, it all stemmed from the handfeeding associating this activity to his stall and surrounding area. Unchecked, it then escalated to the point where he had become dangerous in that particular scenario, which led to protecting his surrounding area.

Each scenario we tried was specifically created to explore different possibilities, aspects, and causes to Hermano's behavior. Through these exercises, we broke down, layer by layer, to uncover the root cause of his behavior. Gradually, in Hermano's own language, he showed us how to place the pieces together to create the full picture. And, as it turned out, he was not, as many had feared, a dangerous horse who could not be trusted in any situation with a concern that he might take his aggression to unknown heights. Instead, we were dealing with a conditioned response, one that could be reconditioned with the help and cooperation of the same people who had unintentionally created the problem in the first place.

11

WOULD YOU TRUST YOU?

REACHOUTTOHORSES.COM

LIFE DOES NOT GET
BETTER BY CHANCE, IT GETS
BETTER BY CHANGE.

"Many times, we are so busy and have such
time-constrained and stressed lives that, despite
our best intentions, we don't see our horses."

When I was asked to write an article about bonding and gaining your horse's trust, my first thought was: "One of the simplest yet hardest things to do. And what makes it hard is not in the horse, but in us."

Many times, we are so busy and have such time-constrained and stressed lives that, despite our best intentions, we don't see our horses. I don't mean they literally vanish into thin air, but we don't see the horse in front of us. Instead, we see what we project onto them.

We don't consider who our horses are, how their day might have been, or what they like or dislike, especially if we haven't had the best of days ourselves. We expect our horses to make us feel better and don't realize that maybe they need us to brighten their day.

If you truly want to create a trust-based partnership with your horse, then you must put down your "tricks of the trade," stop trying to figure out a foolproof technique, and look within yourself. Here are some ways to strengthen trust and begin bonding with your horse, as well as some signs that you are making some progress.

Getting started

Few things will relax and calm your mind like getting in touch with nature—listening to the quiet, enjoying the sun on your skin, or feeling the grass between your toes. We often forget this is where our horses live. They spend every moment being in and of the natural world.

Bonding with your horse in his natural environment is getting to know him as he is. Instead of coming to him with your agenda, try leaving it behind once in a while. Sit down with your horse in the paddock. Watch his motions, his emotions, and his interactions. Find out who he is when he's not being forced to work. Let him discover you on his terms. Allow him to explore you, approach you, and greet you in his own time.

"At times, we expect our horse to make us feel better, not thinking that maybe our horse needs us to brighten their day."

"Getting to know your horse in his natural environment is getting to know him."

Saying "hello"

Have you ever been approached by a boisterous person—loud voice, hard handshake, jumping into your space and demanding your attention? That's not a comfortable experience for most, yet this is often how we greet our horses. We walk right up and put a halter on, or start touching, petting, or grooming, regardless of how the horse feels. Instead, try inviting your horse to the meeting. Notice how he reaches out with his nose as he stretches toward you to discover your uniqueness.

I'm not "comfortable" with that

You wouldn't let another person touch you inappropriately, and your horse feels the same. Ask her and let her invite you into her vulnerable areas before you start poking, prodding, and rubbing. Get her approval to explore her defenseless areas, then you can scratch her withers, rub her body, and search for those special places she likes rubbed. Let her show you what she's comfortable with.

Not only will you introduce yourself further, but you'll be asking your horse to accept you for what you do and not for what you are: a predator. You will also discover her favorite "itchy" areas, making that ever-important good first impression.

About face

Many horses enjoy human contact, while others learn, in time, that it can be comforting. Here are a few common ways horses like to experience human touch around the face. Find the ones your own equine likes in order to deepen the bonding experience.

Ears: Massage his ears. Begin at the base and work your way up to the tip. Discover what he enjoys, and build on the positive experiences. Work in a fluid rhythm, creating circular motions or stroking the ears. There are acupressure points at the tips of the ears that alleviate stress, so many horses just melt into instant relaxation when massaged here.

Eyes: A particularly sensitive nerve center is located right under the horse's eyes. When you move two or three finger pads in the direction of the hairline and create small circles, your horse will begin to relax. Be careful not to use your fingertips, as you may dig your nails into his skin. As you increase the area of the circles, you may be able to cover your horse's eye; and by momentarily taking his vision, you ask him to trust in your protection.

Muzzle: Cup your hand over your horse's muzzle, circle your palm and let him tell you if he likes the cradling feeling or the gentle motion of your hand against his lips. If you're a more advanced horseman or woman, you may wish to place two or three finger pads against the top gum, once again circling as you go.

> *"Asking your horse to drop his head is asking him to give up his primary form of defense: flight."*
>
> *"Horses gain leadership by controlling one another's feet and taking possession of territory. In other words, if you control their forward motion and direction, you take the leadership role in your herd of two."*

Remember to make your way to the front of your horse's mouth by entering the side first. This massage can be very soothing, but be cautious that your horse doesn't pull your fingers between his teeth. The top lip can be very powerful!

Neck drops

For the anxious and frightened horse, this can be the most difficult request. If your horse is willing to drop his head for you, you are well on your way to bonding and gaining his trust. When you ask your horse to do this, you are asking him to give up his primary form of defense: flight.

Anatomically, horses need their heads up high to focus on distance. When their heads are lowered, you remove this ability and ask them to focus on the ground. At that point, their trust has been completely placed in your hands. As a horse lowers his head for you, he presents the most vulnerable part of his body, the back of his neck. This is exactly where a lion would strike to asphyxiate her prey. Some say that crouching down by the side of your horse and encouraging him to lower his eyes below your own takes bonding and trust to an even deeper level.

One way to request a neck drop is to place pressure on the lead rope underneath the clip. The pressure is very slight, equivalent to holding a baby bird. Notice if your horse responds to a constant pressure or if he prefers a pulsing within the pressure. Either way, remember that horses learn from the release of pressure, so your timing in rewarding the tries is crucial to encouraging his nose to touch the ground.

Neck yielding

This exercise offers many advantages, including muscle stretches, tissue softness, natural adjustments, and preparation for the one-rein stop. One of the greatest benefits is that it builds trust. By asking your horse to softly, smoothly, and willingly yield his head around, touching your hipbone farthest from his head, you take away his vision in one eye. Horses are known to follow their noses and this tight neck yield prevents an open and immediate flight path. Losing vision decreases his flight options, a major part of the horse's survival instinct, and asks him to completely place his trust in you.

Disengaging hindquarters

Take a moment to do the following exercise: Stand up, cross your legs, and now . . . run! Okay, stand up again—you probably fell flat on your face. This is exactly what your horse would experience if you made her disengage her hindquarters. When you do this, you take away her ability to run and instead ask her to look to you for guidance.

Horses gain leadership by controlling one another's feet and taking possession of territory. In other words, if you control your horse's forward motion and direction, you take the leadership role in your herd of two. (This takes us into another topic, respect, but we shall save that for another chapter.)

I hope these tips will start you on the path of bonding and building a trust-based relationship with your horse. Remember, it's not about developing the right trust-building techniques and tricks. Your horse is not a motorcycle that always goes on command. He is a living, breathing being, so bonding with him is extremely important. Ask yourself: "Based on my actions and intentions, would I trust me?" Treat him as you would like to be treated. See him for who he is. Be the kind of person he can trust and rely on and you will develop a bond that will never be broken.

Boredom Busting for You and Your Horse

Springtime finds most people getting back in the saddle and preparing horses for trails and competition. The winter, on the other hand, is usually a very different story. As the snow,

Ice, and cold settle in, it can often spoil our best-laid plans. But with a positive attitude and a little creativity we can continue to connect with our equine partners. Five minutes is all it takes!

Here are some boredom-busting and bonding ideas for you and your horse in the winter:

- **GROOMING:** Instead of mindless grooming, focus on mindful grooming; it'll help you connect to one another on a deeper level.

- **TEACH YOUR HORSE A TRICK OR TWO:** A fun way to communicate and connect is to train your horse using enjoyable activities that naturally complement your training program. Think about the value of teaching him to:

   Come when you call
   Pick up a hoof when you click your fingers
   Stretch his front legs (girth stretch) with a mere hand signal

- **COMPANION WALKING:** We all benefit from a breath of fresh air. As you embrace the outdoors with your dog at least twice a day, consider taking your equine partner with you. Make exploring and venturing into nature a family affair.

- **BAREBACK AND BRIDLELESS**: When the weather inhibits trail riding, challenge yourself to return to a true trust-based relationship by removing tack. For effective communication, connect with your horse through your mind and body instead of artificial aids. Explore the power of animal communication and experience the subtleties of a flowing connection.

A chilly time can become a cherished time and a relationship-changing experience, as introspection brings forth unexpected gifts and paves the way for New Year's resolutions that will blossom in the spring.

12

On Swirls and Horses

Many of my clients have bred their horses for the quantity of swirls in support of performance and otherwise. It's an insightful, informative, and intuitive subject and can certainly keep you safe when you meet horses for the very first time, as it gives great insights into their personality and possible behavioral proclivities.

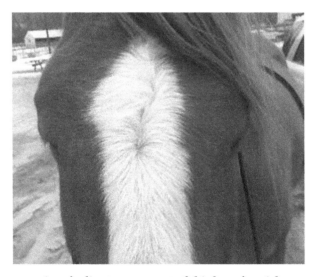

Anna's client assessment of this horse's swirl

Very interesting and not the usual swirl that I have seen. If I am identifying this correctly, the swirl lies slightly to the left, also making her left-side dominant. So I would teach her on the left side first, not because it's standard, but because she would benefit from that side more. Equally, if she has a bad experience on this side, it would show up quickly.

I have found that horses with a "wheat sheaf" swirl (elongated swirl) do not tolerate fools and prefer information to be clear and precise. They are often misunderstood and can find themselves in difficult circumstances, frequently being sold on multiple occasions. When the information is not correctly presented, they are known to have a short fuse and will often "act out." Sometimes this causes major behavioral issues and, as a horse whisperer, I find myself involved to not only save lives but also to act as messenger on their behalf.

Horses appreciate clear messages the first time around with consistency, recognition for their character, strength, and knowledge. Be sure to bring in the sensitivity of the chestnut, as you will be required to be a great leader as you honor your herd of two!

This helps me when I meet horses for the first time and have to be at liberty with them. Often, I only have an hour to "fix" a behavioral issue and I thread my knowledge in for support and safety for sure. If you are asking where this information is coming from, my point of reference is my knowledge and experience, not documented other than in my head at this time.

> **Client's response:** Thank you, Anna! Yes, very helpful. Nevada is scary-smart and insists on clarity and respect in communication. She does have a short fuse, but fortunately her acting out involves mostly a refusal to interact the next day, once you've insulted her or her

intelligence. She's the most intuitive and communicative of my horses, in terms of understanding human
"issues" (equine-guided learning is our job). Much
more than the other two horses, Nevada has facilitated
some major breakthroughs for my clients, in extremely
creative ways. Thanks for your additional insight!

13

Don't Catch Your Horse; Let Your Horse Come to You!

"What is the real reason our horses don't want to be caught? In general, that question can be answered in one sentence: They don't see value in our presence."

"The way you carry yourself gives your horse a great deal of information about you and what is on your mind for the day. If there are time pressures, concerns, or fears, they will know."

I am very fortunate. When I look back over my life, for the most part, I have always wanted to get out of bed, welcome the day, and witness what life has in store for me. It's the thought of those everyday wonders about to happen right in front of my eyes that keeps me excited: seeing the miracles nature has to offer, meeting new people, and experiencing the multitude of cultures all around the globe.

I adore the fact that every experience is an opportunity to learn something new, albeit challenging at times. Each encounter with friends, family. and those around me is a chance to gain and share insights into the life lessons specific to each of us yet shared by all. And if we are paying attention, we can witness the impact trickle down to the next person and the next and the next . . . .

When working with your horse hold on to these types of feelings as best you can, as this is what we want our horses to feel when they see us. We want them to greet us with joy and excitement, asking, "What's in store today?"

For those horses who don't want to be close and run a mile when they see us approach, we have a frustrating challenge on our hands. If we are to solve the problem of "catching a horse that doesn't want to be caught," we have to ask the tough questions and be prepared for the answers no matter what they are. We have to ask what is the "real" reason they don't want to be with us; what is the underlying cause?

Although the specific answers may be varied, in general that question can be answered in one sentence: they don't see value in our presence. But what does this really mean to us? Our horses are trying to tell us something and it's our responsibility to listen and understand. So, it is time to stop trying to catch your horse and instead hear what your horse is saying. If you can change what your horse doesn't like, then you will never have to catch your horse again. Instead, he will greet you with excitement and curiosity.

Discomfort

Before you do anything at all, you need to consider your horse's well-being. As a living, breathing member of the planet, that well-being includes physical, mental, and emotional needs. Your horse may be trying to tell you how he feels physically. He will have begun to change his behavior under saddle, expressed his feelings while being tacked-up, and finally, with no more options available to him, moved on to show you he no longer wants to come to you, as this means he will be subjected to discomfort yet again. So, to start off . . . .

Create a checklist of possibilities:

- Tack-fitting: Saddle, girth, bridle
- Teeth floating: Sharp edges, wolf teeth, abscesses
- Injuries, illnesses and pain: Seek vet advice and then consider a chiropractor, massage therapist, acupuncturist, or energy healer
- Hooves/shoe fitting: consult a farrier
- Rider inability/error: maybe some lessons are in order

Once we take care of any physical pain, we can then look at the possible emotional trauma a horse may have faced in the past. Just like humans, the loss of young, grieving missed friendships, location moves, inappropriate management and handling, and a myriad of other experiences can easily create trauma in a horse. These memories stay with horses for life and it's our commitment that helps them through these troubling experiences.

> **Tip: Consult professional advice to help your horse through any type of trauma or discomfort**

Your Body Language

Like most beings on the planet, including humans, horses' language is primarily non-verbal. They express themselves through body language using gestures, actions, energy, and visualization. They analyze your movements upon approach, intuitively reading your agenda, inner thoughts, feelings, beliefs, and limitations.

The way you carry yourself gives your horse a great deal of information about you and what is on your mind for the day. If there are time pressures, concerns or fears, they will know. Some horses pride themselves on supporting their "guardian" during these situations, while others feel it's best to just not get involved and walk the other way.

> **Tip: Leave your baggage at the gate and don't let it interfere with your horse work.**

Your horse's body language

The horse's language is predictable, discernable and effective. It's a language that can be learned and, although in a horse's eyes we are predators, we can bridge the gap between the two worlds.

"Like most beings on the planet, including humans, horses' language is primarily nonverbal. Even the subtlest of gestures speaks loudly to a horse."

Learn your horse's language. You can't talk to your horse if you don't know what you are saying.

Visualize a plan and be flexible. Don't be afraid to change the goal if it doesn't fit the moment.

Observe horses in their natural habitat and you will witness the intricacies of their communication and interactions. Even the subtlest of gestures speaks loudly to a horse. It's important to remember that when you walk out to the pasture:

Are you yelling at them with your body language or are you whispering to them?

Are you talking to them or talking at them? All types of communication can be valid and useful in the appropriate circumstance.

What is your body language saying and how is it impacting those around you? For example, walking straight at your horse, shoulders pointed toward your horse, eyes piercing your horse's eyes, tells your horse one thing: you mean business. Without realizing it, you have just put pressure on your horse.

You are saying, "Pay attention" or "Leave the area, this is my piece of grass." Either way, your actions demand a response.

Your horse is only too happy to oblige and walk off or, if you are particularly unlucky, this is where the "games" begin!

So how should you approach your horse? Well, horses naturally walk in arcs and at angles. Therefore, it would be more appropriate to approach your horse with a slight curve, creating a half-moon in front of your horse. By remaining in front of your horse's shoulders at all times you are ensuring that you don't inadvertently drive him away.

In addition, rather than strong gestures, horses prefer more passive movements and actions. Try rounded shoulders and soft movements, lowering your head slightly and using your peripheral vision to watch your horse's response. This type of communication tells your horse that you mean no harm.

You can learn more about "the language of Equus" and how to talk to your horse in my DVD series "Reach Out to Natural Horsemanship."

Tip: Learn your horse's language. You can't talk to your horse if you don't know what you are saying.

Your Agenda

Not only do horses read our body language, they also know our agendas. For us this means we need to pay particular attention to our thoughts. It's a great idea to have a goal in mind, but it's also foolish to fall in love with it! Stay in the moment as you communicate with your equine partner and don't be afraid to change your mind if your original plan doesn't seem to fit the moment.

Tip: Visualize a plan and be flexible. Don't be afraid to change the goal if it doesn't fit the moment.

Your horse's feelings

You may need to examine your agenda in greater depth. Consider all the times you visit your horse:

Are there occasions when you need to let off steam, tack up and enjoy the countryside, visit your friends, or improve your riding skills?

Does each visit involve only your needs and happiness or do you include how your horse feels on this particular day? If each time you visit you don't see his needs, he will begin to walk away regardless of what you need.

We have all occasionally woken up on the wrong side of the bed. Maybe your horse is having a bad day too. He could have been scolded by another horse, missed breakfast or lunch, disliked cold weather, merely be tired from a bad night's sleep, or feel a little sore.

If you are not in a position to board your horse at home, remember to ask those who take care of him. They may know more.

Tip: Keep the channels of communication open. Give your horse a voice in your plans.

Motivation

Motivation is the key for your horse to want to come to you; you are partners, after all. What motivates your horse? Nearly everyone likes to assume, and I hear common answers like "food" or "rest," but it's not until we let our horse tell us that we will know for sure.

During the Reach Out to Horses Certification program, all students get together on the last day to discover just this. We wait until later in the program to ensure we have some background knowledge on individual horses, as this exercise can become somewhat precarious otherwise. I suggest you only venture down this road if you have the right equipment and always make safety your first priority. You can also adapt the exercise to suit your needs.

Exercise:

Equipment: Safety helmet, gloves, long-line, and halter.

Duration: The exercise lasts about twenty to thirty minutes, and students are assigned their specific horse for the week.

Prior to starting the exercise, it is fun to write down what you think motivates your horse!

1. Clip the long-line onto the halter with about twenty to twenty-five feet in the line, so your horse has plenty of room to explore.

2. Without hinting or guiding your horse, allow him to show you what intrigues him. This will give you a chance to explore his true motivation. It's important to stay safe throughout the exercise and remain at a forty-five-degree angle without stepping into the kick zone. Although some horses have picked up a jog, it's best to keep the exercise calm and slow.

Keep the channels of communication open.
Give your horse a voice in your plans.

Once you discover your horse's preferences you are
in a position to praise accordingly.

The more time you spend with your horse, the more
time you'll have spent with him, strengthening
your bond and creating a great partnership.

Each time we conduct this exercise, students come back surprised with the results. Some horses explore every stall and opening, others visit all the horses on the property. Individuals have pranced, displaying their manhood, while others have shared the joy of grazing.

Once you discover your horse's preferences, you are in a position to praise accordingly. By building that motivation into your personal program, you give your horse a voice too!

Tip: Discover what motivates your horse and incorporate it into the time with him.

Hopefully you can now see why there is no such thing as: "I can't catch my horse." Investing the time to listen to and understand your horse will reap rewards far beyond being able to catch him in the pasture. Plus, the more time you spend with your horse, the more time you'll have spent with him, strengthening your bond and creating a great partnership. And, after all, isn't that the reason you got him in the first place?

14

THE SELF-LOADING HORSE

Greatness is not what you have ...

It's what you give.

"You may have heard the idea that 'preparation and planning prevent poor performance.' This couldn't be truer for trailer loading as well."

"Act like you have all day and it will take you ten minutes."

"Shoulda, coulda, woulda" describes the strategies of many when it comes to loading their horse into the trailer. Not until the day creeps upon us do we realize just how important trailer-loading practice can be—for us and for our horses.

You may have heard the idea that "preparation and planning prevent poor performance." This couldn't be truer for trailer loading as well. We often think we don't have time to practice loading with our horse. But in actuality, the reality is just the opposite: you don't have time to not practice trailer loading. By taking that time, in the long run, you will not only save time but save yourself future frustrations and time pressures. And possibly—even more importantly—you are creating and strengthening the bond and trust-based relationship between you and your horse.

As part of a clear plan, take an active part in your horse's education and welfare. As his guardian, it behooves you both to understand how your horse's mind ticks.

Myths:

"Bribe your horse!" – Horses are not predators, meaning they have never needed to hunt for their food, kill prey, and then reap the reward. Their food is right underfoot! Therefore, although they do see value in food for comfort and nourishment, they do not see the same value as other species in gaining food for reward.

"Drag or push him into the trailer!" – Horses are "into pressure" beings. This phenomenon has developed over 54 million years and forms part of their survival trait. They lean into anything they perceive to be pressure in order to protect themselves. If not taught to come off pressure, they will raise their heads up high, lean backward, stop, or even run in the opposite direction. So, pushing or pulling only enhances their suspicions and behavior patterns.

"Put the ramp up quickly!" – This is the worst thing you can do once your horse has loaded. Horses are naturally claustrophobic; so, by closing the ramp before your horse is comfortable, you will create additional pressure and not allow them the freedom to experience a release of pressure. Instead, let them leave and reenter the trailer again and again. This way, your horse will gain confidence and comfort both in and out of the trailer.

Helpful Hints:

"Act like you have all day and it will take you ten minutes." Remove all time constraints on the day of loading and stay calm and relaxed. Your horse reads your intentions, agenda, and emotions. Let him see that you are not under pressure. If you are nervous or under pressure, consider utilizing flower remedies or aromatherapy oils for both of you. Lavender is an old faithful!

"Friends don't let friends struggle." – Trailer loading can be a tricky task. Bring a friend along until you feel comfortable to load your horse alone. You may ask them to close the ramp behind you (if you have a jockey door) or hold onto the rope through the window as you prepare your horse for the trip. This isn't the time to be a hero!

". . . and they came two by two." – There was a reason Noah loaded all of his animals in twos! If your horse travels better with his/her partner, why not bring them along for the day?

"It's bright, shiny and new." – You may be proud of how clean and perfect your brand-new trailer looks, but horses are suspicious of new trailers, as they aren't used to the sights and smells of an artificial shiny metal container. Many may be reluctant to take that first step, so instead of making him face this stressful situation alone, try taking another horse along. Having "old faithful" by his side might be just what your horse needs to feel more comfortable in this uncomfortable situation.

"Remember that rather hairy last trip?" – Well, so do our four-legged companions. Except for them it would have been even more adventurous in the back of the trailer. They don't forget their last experience, so you need to drive carefully and always take their comfort into account.

"He loaded just fine at home." – Horses are associative thinkers. They associate specific events with locations. Imagine individual pictures formulating a movie, this is the creation of a horse's memory. Take each lesson to new places so your horse learns to load in any given location—five is often the magic number!

Our horses might be saying:

"Be aware of your body language" – You could be giving your horse the wrong message. Are you hesitating on the ramp? Are you looking your horse in his eyes? Are you expecting him to refuse? These thoughts and gestures all indicate to your horse that it's best he steers clear of the trailer.

"Don't wait until we do something wrong, reward us for doing something right."

"The art of listening to your horse is to capture his thoughts and reward him in a timely fashion."

Replace all of your negative or anxious thoughts with positive ones. Act like your horse loads every time. This image not only transfers to your horse telepathically but is also received energetically down the line and is reflected physically in your body language and movements.

"Eyes are the window to the soul." – you can hide behind a smile, but you can't hide behind your eyes. They reflect your true emotions. At the same time, if you look your horse in the eyes throughout a loading session, you are communicating to him in his language to stand and not come to you. Think about the times you have witnessed your horse speak to another horse—the first gesture they make connects them to one another through eye contact. They often follow this with a reprimand, guidance, or a request. Couple this with your posture or a hesitation in your footfall and you are relaying to your partner to stand still or be concerned with what is coming.

Try placing your eyes on your horse's chest or feet to read their next thought. You can also use your peripheral vision to watch their facial expressions to gain insights into their thoughts.

Horses drag their eyes, rather than snapping them onto new objects as humans do. Consider dragging your eyes to where you would like your horse to come.

"Don't wait until we do something wrong, reward us for doing something right." – We have a window of three- to eight-tenths of a second to reward our horse for trying. It's within this window that he associates your reward with the

88 | Beyond the Barn

action. The art of listening to your horse is to capture his thoughts and reward him in a timely fashion.

Look for the change in his eye, the flick of his ear, the swish of his tail, and the muscle movement. As your horse is about to perform, stay out of his way.

Recognize the tries. Tries might be:

- The glance toward the trailer
- Interest in the trailer
- Reaching out toward the ramp
- Changing his weight and leaning inward
- Smelling the ramp and inside
- Relaxing his jaw and facial muscles
- Coming off pressure
- Lifting his foot

Discover what your horse perceives as reward. Is it the rub on the forehead or the neck, the release of physical pressure, your soothing voice, a pulsing pressure, or just pure rest? Build in different rewards so that there is clarity between desirable and undesirable behavior.

"We work off the path of least resistance."

Horses move away from discomfort into comfort. The easiest and fastest way to teach a horse to stand would be to ask for forward motion with the pressure halter, gain no response, and return to rub your horse on the forehead. By doing this you are reinforcing standing.

Create clear boundaries for desirable and undesirable behavior and an environment that encourages your horse to want to learn and create consequences for his actions. For example, if your horse moves off to one side—hiding against the wall of the trailer and you go to get him, reassuring him every step of the way—what you have done in fact is the following:

- Missed his thought of avoiding forward motion
- Allowed him to control his feet
- Created an easier option/exit than actually facing his fear
- Released the constant pressure
- Created rest around the corner
- Rubbed him for his clever thought
- Encouraged him for finding this path of least resistance

The path of least resistance should always be the direction and task you have in mind for him to complete.

"Direct my nose." – Horses follow their noses! Not only will this allow you and your horse to keep your eye on the target it will also create focus. As your horse learns to maintain attention he equally learns about the path of least resistance.

By capturing the whisper, you will be able to guide him to his final destination.

Follow these simple tips and you will not only save time and aggravation but, most importantly, you'll build your horse's confidence and comfort level around the trailer. And the next time you have to take a trip your horse might just walk right in on his own.

Seeing Eye to Eye

If horses had their own school, they would break down every physical exercise they learned into two sections: left-side practice and right-side practice. Unlike humans, who gain and process information through both eyes simultaneously, horses don't process that same amount of information from the left to the right side of the brain. When you pick up a glass with your left hand, for instance, your right side is very aware that you're holding a glass. That is not necessarily true with a horse.

The amount of information transferred varies from one horse to another and the percentage of information recorded alters depending on what study you read. What is certain though is that horses need time to learn and get comfortable with new objects and items out of both eyes. So, de-sensitize your horse on her comfortable side first to make it easier for her. Once that has been attained, move over to the other side and repeat the process until she is able to accept the item in a relaxed fashion.

Remember, your aim is not to induce flight, but rather to keep your horse calm so she can process the information. If her adrenaline is up, then her learning curve will be down.

15

SPOOK-BUSTING SECRETS

The Living Moment
Is Everything

reachouttohorses.com

Having worked with thousands of horses, here are five keys I've learned to help you desensitize your horse to just about anything you might encounter.

1. Think Ahead

Don't wait for the trail or the show to begin desensitizing your horse. By then, it's too late. Instead, build an obstacle course in the safe environment of your arena. Be creative by including things your horse hasn't seen yet like streamers, mattresses, balloons, golf carts, silly string, sparklers, and horns.

2. Relaxation is Key

Strive to keep your horse relaxed throughout the entire lesson. **Don't bring up the adrenaline-induced flight response, as**

the fear created will make it harder for your horse to retain the information. Try preparing you horse before the lesson with relaxation exercises: ear/eye-and- mouth massages, neck drops, and neck yields. Horses are an "into pressure species," so teach your horse to naturally release himself from pressure on his poll, nose, and head before venturing into the "spook-busting" lesson.

3. Seeing is Believing

Professional athletes use visualization, so why shouldn't you? Preparing mentally and emotionally will help you better handle any situation you might encounter. **Visualize the session from start to finish and imagine the outcome you want to create.** Your visualized intentions and body language will have a direct effect on your horse.

4. Magic Number Three

Horses can learn good (and bad) behavior in only three tries. Additionally, for your horse to associate a negative or positive response to a particular action or event, the reinforcement needs to occur in an optimum time frame of between three- and eight-tenths of a second. Not a lot of time; so make sure your timing is praising the right action.

5. Location, Location, Location . . .

Horses associate behavior patterns, actions, and situations with the place they first experienced them. Take your lessons to several different locations and shake things up a bit to help your horse lose the unintended association and gain a complete spook-busting experience. Solidify your efforts by changing the environment from one location to another; for example, you may begin in the safety of the round pen before expanding your lesson to a larger enclosure such as the arena. From the arena venture to a grassy area or paddock, and eventually increase the stimulus to graduate to the show ring. Thus, your horse no longer associates the experience with a single isolated exercise, but instead has expanded his association and knowledge to encompass several different locations.

16

DE-SPOOKING ISN'T THAT SCARY

Step 1: Recognize the Try

Step 2: Acknowledge the Try

Step 3: Reward the Try

"Often a horse's behavior though can be understood and explained with one simple phrase—horses are, by their very nature, flight animals."

"My mare lies down, trembling, when she gets frightened." Has this ever happened to you? How about "He has jumped on top of me several times when he sees the scooter"? In my travels each year, as I meet hundreds of horses and their human companions from around the globe, these statements and ones just like them are far too common. Dealing with a frightened horse can be frustrating, difficult, and, at times, just as terrifying for the human as it is for the horse.

Often a horse's behavior though can be understood and explained with one simple phrase—horses are, by their very nature, flight animals. Once you understand this idea, desensitizing your horse to almost anything becomes easier and can actually be fun for both you and your horse.

Now is the perfect time to prepare your horse for the many possibly frightening things he may come across in your upcoming adventures together. Too many people wait until after they are out on the trail or at the show to train their horse. Or worse, they don't take the time to expose their horse to enough stimuli beforehand and are suddenly faced with a potentially dangerous situation of new "scary" experiences.

Even the well-seasoned dressage horse, show-jumpers, western pleasure, and performance horses in general, have all been faced with the barking dog, chasing them down the trail, the plastic bag, blowing in the wind, or that loud car that almost seems to sneak up behind you to maximize its startling effect. The more prepared you and your horse are for those unexpected moments, the better chance you have of dealing with them without the bolting, rearing, bucking, and all the rest of the behavior that can make horsemanship so dangerous.

I once conducted a Reach Out to Horses Introductory Course, where we worked, in depth, with the art of "de-spooking," as it is sometimes called. One very effective tool I used during the course (and all the time when desensitizing my horses) is the tarpaulin or "tarp." As many of you know, there is just nothing like it. The crackling sound, the intimidating

size, and odd, unnatural feel scares most horses right out of
their hooves!

---

*Acknowledgement is very important when desensitizing
your horse. Whether it comes in the form of a release
of pressure, removal of direct pressure on the noseband,
soothing and comforting words, or a rub on the forehead,
acknowledging your horse's tries and successes will
help to give him the confidence he needs while facing
this new challenge."*

Using the tarp as a desensitizing tool can be quite a challenge, so I would recommend you just throw it on your horse
or your horse on it. In an ideal situation, I always recommend
that people "Reach Out" to their horse in a round pen environment as the first step before they attempt to introduce any
new stimuli. "Reaching out" to your horse is a unique experience. During this process you communicate in the non-verbal
language of the horse. By adopting the gestures and movements already familiar to your horse, you begin to create a
trust-based partnership from the ground up.

Reaching out is invaluable to the training. It allows you to:

- Get an instant, physical assessment of your horse's
  abilities
- Determine conformation, personal limitations,
  and what is natural to the breed
- Discover immediate insights into your horse's
  personality and character traits

- Learn your horse's likes, dislikes, needs, willingness, sensitivity, and concentration level
- Communicate, connect, and collaborate
- Dialogue instead of dictate
- Become acquainted

In short, it's an opportunity to create a relationship based on mutual understanding and respect in a safe environment for both you and your horse.

During the course, one of the participants, Tina, used the Reach Out process with her horse, Prophet. In the beginning, Tina took time to introduce herself by conducting a number of "getting to know you" exercises involving relaxation techniques, head-drops, and neck yielding. Prophet was already accustomed to a pressure halter (another invaluable tool when introducing horses to new objects) and by taking a few moments to teach him pressure and release, Tina saved time and possible future conflicts.

When the time was right, Tina let Prophet explore the tarp. Horses, curious by nature, will usually want to examine new objects, cautiously smelling them and feeling them with their feet as they go. With his limited depth perception, Prophet was able to examine the texture of the tarp and realized that unlike water, his feet weren't about to be swallowed all the way up to his knees! Tina then brought Prophet around to approach the tarp on the side he found the easiest—acknowledging his tries along the way.

Acknowledgment is very important when desensitizing your horse. Whether it comes in the form of a release of pressure, removal of direct pressure on the noseband, soothing and comforting words, or a rub on the forehead, acknowledging your horse's tries and successes will help to give him the confidence he needs while facing this new challenge. In addition, horses learn from the release of pressure, so you can use the rewards individually or all at once.

Once Prophet became more comfortable with this new experience, Tina approached the tarp from the opposite direction. Knowing that horses process only part of the information from the right to the left side of the brain, Tina knew that Prophet would need to experience this as a new event to create a complete picture.

"Don't wait for them to get overwhelmed and run from you! If you stop before that moment, to eliminate flight, fight, or freeze, you'll replace it with confidence and comfort."

Folding the tarp so that it's small enough to rub her horse all over was the next important step. She rubbed Prophet with the tarp, covering his entire body, gradually increasing the size of the tarp. Tina was able to quickly discover how Prophet felt about it changing shape and touching his body. Remember to reward the smallest tries—the desired response of standing still and calm. Don't wait for them to get overwhelmed and run from you! If you stop before that moment, to eliminate flight, fight, or freeze, you'll replace it with confidence and comfort.

Finally, Tina asked Prophet to completely relax by lowering his head. She taught him this relaxation technique at the beginning, and even with additional stimulus he understood her request. Horses need to carry their heads high to see far in the distance in order to negotiate their flight path. When you take away their primary form of defense, you ask for an enormous amount of trust. This final offering became the perfect note to finish the lesson.

Once you and your horse mastered the tarp, there are so many other objects to explore with your horse. Don't be afraid to ask a friend for help; it can be safer and a lot more fun when you've got a partner to help you through it. But ultimately, if you remember the golden rule, that horses are, by nature, flight animals, you'll be able to approach de-spooking from a whole different perspective, help your horse overcome even his worst fears, and, more importantly, you'll become the genuine leader of the trust-based herd of two!

17

To Whip or Not to Whip

Hatred and anger speak twice as loud as **tolerance and kindness**, so tolerance and kindness must speak TWICE as often.

REACHOUTTOHORSES.COM

"I don't want to exacerbate the issue," my client pronounced a few hours prior to her private lesson with me. She expressed concern that the desensitizing lesson may be less than helpful to her at a time when she needed it most to progress to the next level of dressage, involving a high-level movement called piaffe. For now, she was at a standstill. I assured her that our lesson would not harm but only enhance her relationship with her Andalusian stallion and that she would be present throughout the whole session.

A small group gathered just moments prior to what was supposed to be our private consultation as word had leaked out among the whole dressage barn. My briefing included a small synopsis that Madrid was passionately concerned with the dressage whip and no-one could get near him with the whip without him freaking out and running backward or spinning, leaving the scene absolutely out of control. It was believed that his former guardians had chased him with the whip on the continent from which he came.

Madrid was led into the outside round pen where we introduced ourselves to one another. I was confident that he was familiar with my methods of "reaching out," together with the halter work in preparation for him to release himself from pressure, because all barn staff had been trained to my methods over the past five years. He appeared very calm and relaxed in an environment he was used to. In order to assess the situation, it was important for me to break each step down into bite-sized chunks. This way I would be able to come to an educated conclusion as to Madrid's cause of fear.

Hints and Tips

I began simply by approaching Madrid, stroking him with my hand on the shoulder, neck, or head, and subsequently walking away from him, thereby enforcing his appropriate behavior of standing quietly. With each approach, I changed my speed, mannerism, angle of approach and body language, but at all times remained calm.

The next step included taking the whip with me, stroking him on the shoulder and praising him; through the release of walking away and a soothing voice. During this particular training session, I actually included the use of food as reward. This decision was based on the deep-rooted cause and extended period of time the barn had been experiencing the behavior pattern. The bucket of carrots was left on the outside of the round pen so that Madrid would not associate me as the carrot dispenser. It's a safe way to ensure there would be no mugging. Each time I walked away from him with the whip in hand I returned just moments later with a bucket of carrots for him to choose from. He was allowed to dip his nose into the bucket and choose a mouthful of carrot, but just one.

If at any time he thought he could not cope and needed to leave, we saw this response through tension in his body and would take the lesson slower.

We continuously reminded him that he would not be harmed, but instead that he would be able to exchange his past experiences for positive memories.

I suggested my rider stay very focused and clear with her requests, not allowing for any preconceived ideas so that the messages and pictures she had in her mind would represent the outcome she desired.

I was sure to introduce the experience of the whip touching him from each side of his body and out of both eyes, thereby giving Madrid two separate visual experiences. **Within a short time frame, Madrid realized that he was in full control of this whip and could direct it at all times by his stillness alone.**

As Madrid proved that he was able to process this portion of the lesson completely without any signs of fear, flight, or fight, it was time to tack him up to initiate a normal riding lesson. We repeated the exercise of approach and retreat, praising each and every try Madrid made. If at any time he thought he could not cope and needed to leave, we saw this response through tension in his body and would take the lesson slower. However, we "raised the bar" to include a mounting block as height for him to view the whip from below, continuously reminding him that he would not be harmed, but instead that he would be able to exchange his past experiences for positive memories.

At the suggestion of my client, we brought Madrid's trainer into the round pen to mount him, because it was in this moment in the past that a whip could not be passed to the rider. Now, fully tacked, Madrid's trainer was given the full use of her reins as we clipped on the pressure halter to keep everyone safe. The audience went quiet and you could hear the drop of a pin. As I approached Madrid with the whip, he stood like a rock for me to pass the whip to his rider. Immediately I took the whip back and walked away. We gave him time and space to process the last request before we began to repeat the exercise on both sides of his body without any adverse reactions. Instead of praising each increment step with food, we now offered the carrots for greater achievements.

Observing Madrid's body language throughout this whole exchange allowed us to move forward and I asked his male trainer to join us, to see if this would trigger any past incidents from his previous life. Believing that we had placed a good foundation on Madrid, it was time for him to graduate and stand by himself with his rider aboard in the round pen. The attached line and grounds person were removed, for Madrid to process the upcoming movements by himself. Imagine our delight when the trainer was able to just walk up to Madrid as though he had approached him a thousand times before and hand the whip to the rider!

He was totally aware that the whip represented a good feeling and that something positive would follow just shortly after. It was truly magical to observe.

Although I was taken aback by how much Madrid was able to absorb and I was proud of his courage and progress, this was to be just the beginning. My client was astounded and yet believed that maybe the arena was the cause to all the problems and we should, in fact, take the lesson inside. It was quite possible that Madrid would associate the whip with the indoor arena and not the outside round pen. Quite a lot of information had been gathered in the first half of the lesson for us to now move into a more "pressured" situation.

I was informed that one of the most complicated tasks was to ride up to the side of the arena and reach for the whip. Please know that the whip was only to be used as an aid in preparing Madrid for the finer cues needed to attain piaffe and not as a form of punishment. I suggested they show me how they approach the side for me to witness the manner of the approach and possible outcome. Madrid was ridden straight up to the ledge where his rider reached for the whip and he stood calmly. "He is going to make a liar out of me yet," she said with a broad smile on her face as Madrid stood without moving even a single step. We repeated this approach several times and from many different angles.

I suggested my rider stay very focused and clear with her requests, not allowing for any preconceived ideas so that the messages and pictures she had in her mind would represent the outcome she desired. We continued to praise all of Madrid's efforts through petting his neck, soothing words, walking away from the ledge, and the occasional mouthful of carrots to reinforce our message. Within just moments Madrid began to aim for the ledge to touch the whip on his own accord. He was totally aware that the whip represented a good feeling and that something positive would follow just shortly after. It was truly magical to observe.

It was suggested that we incorporate some training prior to reaching for the whip. That Madrid be "worked" as though he was in a lesson to stimulate his body and mind. That possibly the change in rhythm and focus would cause his concerns and yet Madrid took this together with all the other lessons in stride. He was clearly graduating from each one of his lessons.

There was just one incident, one spook, where I got to witness the fear in Madrid's eye. Our intention was for the rider to create small circles at the trot, slowing down, and coming to a stop for our handler to pass the whip across to her. When we reached this point, Madrid ran side-ways while backing away from the whip, each step faster than the other. Madrid's rider just settled with his movements, allowing him the space to gather his thoughts before she asked him once again to approach our ground-person. This time he was able to absorb any kind of fear and we were able to reinforce our positive lessons. It's at times like these we can take a step backward to go forward. We repeated some of the positive lessons he was able to perform to give him the confidence he needed to proceed.

Sometimes we can take a step backward to go forward. We repeated some of the positive lessons he was able to perform to give him the confidence he needed to proceed.

He would learn that the whip was indeed an aid and not a form of punishment; he would come to understand the proper use of the whip.

It dawned on me at that moment that Madrid was not frightened of the whip but was indeed frightened of when it appeared—the timing of the introduction to the whip. Each time the whip had been introduced was when Madrid had tried to comprehend a request but was not processing it correctly. Our rider intended to utilize the whip for clarity of an aid, and yet

Madrid thought it would be presented as punishment. Although he had tried hard to understand, he knew that he had not understood the request and believed the whip was on hand as it had been in his past—to tell him off, to show him how bad he had been. It all became clear. I suggested to my client that she introduce the whip earlier in her future lessons, while he was still in a relaxed state and before any signs of confusion. That way, he would learn that the whip was indeed an aid and not a form of punishment; he would come to understand the proper use of the whip.

We continued with our lesson for just a few moments longer, finishing on a perfect note at just under ninety minutes. Madrid readily accepted the positioning our ground-person who it took to begin to introduce him to the first movements of piaffe. She gently held his rein in her left hand, guiding his nose and neck carriage, while carrying the whip in the right hand, gently tapping him on his rear end. It was a picture to be seen. Horse and rider in harmony with one another. In the whole time his person had known Madrid, she had not been able to pick up a whip without an adverse reaction, let alone able to get the handler to come within ten feet of Madrid. Now he was accepting both the handler and the whip as he digested the information presented to him. I have no doubt Madrid will make it to the next dressage level and I look forward to seeing him in the show ring upon my next trip!

Opening Up Communication

Communication consists of body language, energy inter-action, interspecies communication, and probably much more that we don't know about.

Learning to listen to our horses is the first part of learning to communicate with them. Learning to respond and to request comes second. After studying horses' body language, behavior, interaction, and herd hierarchy, we can now speak with them through our own body language, gestures, and even our intentions. Anyone can learn this language, but fluency requires patience, practice, and time spent observing the native speakers.

Remember, in any language, only 7 percent is verbal. Eye contact makes up 13 percent of a language while about 80 percent comes from non-verbal cues, including facial expressions, gestures, posture, physical proximity, and physical contact. So, be aware of what you project to your horse.

18

REACH OUT TO HORSES

"*Not only can horses read the body language of every member of their species, they can read humans just as easily. They can, almost immediately, see your agenda and how you are feeling.*"

Horses have walked the Earth for more than 54 million years. While some do not consider them among the brightest of the animal kingdom, most are unaware that through their lengthy tenure on this planet they have created an effective non-verbal language that some have coined "the language of Equus." This is a language that goes well beyond the unspoken. Through careful observation, humans have been able to interpret and adopt this method of communication.

Originating from the horses' body language, behavior, interaction, and herd hierarchy, humans can now speak with them through our own body language, gestures, and even our intentions. This language, like any, requires patience and practice. It can be taught to anyone, but fluency only comes from time spent observing and communicating with the native speakers.

Not only can horses read the body language of every member of their species they can read humans just as easily. They can, almost immediately, see your agenda and how you are feeling. They will highlight your strengths and weaknesses. In effect, they know who you are and what that means to them in a very short period of time. You can lie to yourself but you can't lie to a horse. Therefore, it's important that you begin every interaction with a clear mind, leaving "all your baggage" at the gate.

One place to start the conversation with your horse is the round pen. Using the round pen as your classroom can be very helpful in creating a trust-based relationship. This type of conversation is the foundation to all interaction, every ground session, ridden work, and ultimately your success. A fifty-foot round pen is suggested as it allows free motion for horses of most sizes. It's also important to make sure you have appropriate footing, which is essential to maintaining health and fitness.

"Remember that communication takes place whenever you are together. Each motion and gesture you make says something to your four-legged partner."

This is an example of a typical session in the round pen. It's important to note that this is an overview and is not intended to be a formula or a "quick fix" to solve behavioral issues, and it requires dedication and commitment to learn and apply. Remember that communication takes place whenever you are together. Each gesture and motion you make says something to your four- legged partner.

Familiarization: Horses need the chance to explore the round pen at liberty. They naturally check out their perimeters, take time to settle and to explore the vicinity through their senses. Each horse is an individual and as such will react in different ways to different circumstances. This 15- to 20-minute period is an ideal time to observe its character and learn to read its personality.

Orientation: This is the official introduction and there are many important steps in this portion which include:

First Impressions
The introduction to the four directions (north, south, east, and west) of the round pen
Understanding one another's intentions
Energetic and telepathic exchange
Exploration of Dually halter and pressure/release
Body language exchange

Ground manners and pain assessment
The opportunity for handler to read horse
    and horse to read handler
The time for the adrenaline of horse and handler
    to subside
Creation of a comfort zone in the center of
    the round pen
Creation of a safe distance between horse and handler
Influence of speed and direction by the handler
    to gain leadership
Relaxation and intimacy

Communication: In a natural herd environment hierarchy is determined through many factors, one being the manipulation of speed and direction. As mentioned in the orientation process the handler adopts this practice in the round pen environment. The connection between horse and handler takes place before or during the orientation, with a herd of two being formed. Once the herd has been formed and the orientation has been completed the handler asks the horse to leave by driving him away using body language. This is the time to make character assessments, to complete a health check, and to begin forming the partnership with the horse.

A higher-ranking horse will use his body language to communicate or punish another by sending it out of the herd. This gives a strong message, as banishment is a grave risk to their survival.

Through the position the handler takes of driving the horse forward, he will retreat. This is a form of advance and retreat, also known as pressure release and has been used by horsemen for centuries. The handler then adopts equine body language by squaring her shoulders, placing her eyes on the horse's eyes, and advancing forward in an assertive manner. The combination of proximity, speed, movements, and eye contact can mean a number of different things.

As prey animals, horses naturally run for a quarter to three-eighths of a mile before they stop to assess what made them flee. This distance is roughly translated to seven or eight revolutions in the round pen. The fleeing that is induced should not be through fear, but rather a request for forward motion. The trainer takes possession of any area the horse stands in at any given moment gaining leadership. A speed slightly beyond their natural gait is best and will often be in the form of a canter.

When it feels like the right time to change direction, the horse is asked to change direction toward the round pen wall through the trainer's body positioning. The same process of asking the horse to leave is repeated in this direction. Unlike humans, horses only transfer about 20 to 50 percent of all information from the left to the right side of the brain and as such they consider this to be new ground that they are exploring.

Once the horse has explored both directions he is then asked to return to familiar ground, pressure is reduced, but an active involvement is maintained. An assertive walk forward is continued, while allowing the horse to reduce his speed and maintain focus and attention. The trainer's body language becomes a little softer as his intention changes. This procedure is also helpful because the horse will often reveal his history during this time.

The horse will begin to communicate his desire to return to the herd of two. He will relay very clears signs, such as reducing the size of his circle, relaxing his jaw and neck and many other gestures that require some study for the handler to recognize. These are all desired responses, which need acknowledgment through a release of pressure resembling a drop of the eyes, a relaxing of shoulders, slowing of the walk, or a hesitating in the line throwing. This is what makes it a conversation, rather than a demand or a talking at the horse. Each try by the horse should be acknowledged in this manner. Overall, the handler is looking for a complete feeling of unity and a commitment from the horse prior to inviting it back to the herd. This will come with experience and the whole of the "Reach Out" process generally should take no longer than fifteen to twenty minutes.

Reach Out to Horses: A suitable moment is identified to invite the horse to become part of the team again. The invitation takes the form of a sweeping motion in front of the horse and is similar to the natural gesture of displaying one's flank, while eating. The passive nature of the maneuver asks the horse to slow down and step closer. He will choose to stay close to the wall, come part of the way, or come all the way to the handler. If the communication is done correctly but the horse does not return to the handler this may possibly point to a problem, issue, or habit the horse developed before the session. Ultimately, the greatest compliment is that the horse comes up to the handler and reaches out toward her with his nose!

Close Connection: An invitation to the horse is given to come into the heart space where he receives lots of reward and reassurance—creating a close connection. A rub on the forehead will reinforce his positive behavior. The ultimate reward for a horse is the release of pressure, which translates to walking away. Horses naturally move in arcs and angles so, when the time is right, the handler walks away in a clockwise direction to perform a figure of eight. The qualities of a leader are displayed to bring the horse back to the center of the round pen, which becomes a familiar comfort zone.

"Creating this trust-based relationship with your horse can be a magical experience and the moment you feel true partnership is a moment that you will never forget."

Reaching out to your horse is the foundation to all communication. It can take on many forms and will allow you to learn to read and communicate with your horse, while building a trust-based relationship. It is the beginning to all success and will aid in improving existing relationships, embarking on new partnerships, and assessing character and health. From here you can lead into starting young horses, problem solving, improving ground manners, teaching to lead and load, eliminate kicking, biting, and rearing, just to name a few. Creating this trust-based relationship with your horse can be a magical experience and the moment you feel that true partnership is a moment you will never forget.

19

UNCOVERING THE ART OF LONG-LINING

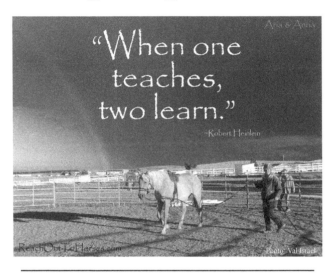

"When one teaches, two learn."
~Robert Heinlein

Always remember that you should already be experienced with long-lining horses who are older and wiser before you venture into starting a young horse under saddle. It is really not advisable to put a green horse with a green handler, as green and green makes black and blue!

We all have passions in life. When it comes to the world of horses there are countless facets to grab our attention and our time. Some may enjoy riding or training. Others might appreciate that daily grooming or feeding time. Still others might appreciate those quiet moments—just you, the horse and stillness. I enjoy all of those but one way of connecting with my horse that I also enjoy, and one that is often overlooked, is through long-lining. For me, there is nothing like reading your horse to create a well-thought-out lesson plan to make both horse and human feel great!

Now you may be wondering if long-lining applies to you directly; after all, it is quite the forgotten art. But once you realize its true benefits, you will certainly want to build it into your routine. Long-lining has often been described as "riding from the ground" and brings with it a multitude of advantages.

Young and un-started horses

On a single day, I started my young Spanish Mustang under saddle. Within an hour, Excalibur accepted his first saddle, bridle, and rider, with complete understanding and willingness. (X had never been ridden with a bit, but this allowed him to feel the sensation.) Admittedly, we had spent eighteen months getting to know one another, but the exercises he experienced that particular day were new to him, long-lining included.

In preparation for his "big day," X had practiced a number of exercises pertaining to long-lining, including neck yields, single-line yielding, head-drops, and disengaging the hindquarters. We began our session by "reaching out" to one another, which established clear communication and created a mutual understanding for the upcoming event.

Without hesitation, and yet showing great interest, X accepted his first saddle, displaying extreme signs of relaxation as he wandered around the round pen with his neck stretched to the ground. The most difficult request that day was to convince X that he needed to explore the saddle and his environment at a slightly more engaging speed! He appeared so settled and trusting that he felt little need to distrust the saddle, even though it was now fixed to his back and hugging his stomach.

Having saved this moment for my students to appreciate, it was clear to me that they were wondering how I would stimulate forward motion at this point. Knowing that X had no fear of the "flag" and yet that he would respect this tool, I opted to create motivation through visual stimulus. My intention was to allow X to explore all three gaits with his new saddle and even though he felt content it was extremely important that he experienced the sensations of this equipment through different muscle movements.

The goal was achieved very quickly and gave me the opportunity to see that X did not consider this to be a challenge of any kind. So, instead of boring him in what was our joint classroom, we raised the bar. Now, it was time to try the long-lines. With both lines attached, X was asked to choose in which direction he preferred to explore the long-lines (which were attached to the halter), and become accustomed to feeling them along his sides, hocks, and body.

At first, this new sensation can desensitize a horse to the motion of lines and the signals you are sending. At times, horses may even stop when they feel this sensation, for when they stop so does the movement. **Encouraging them forward without fear and force is the key.**

I believe the long-lines are one of the best ways to introduce our young horses to pressure on the face/nose or bit. This creates a safe environment for them to learn left, right, forward, slow and stop. **In the highly sensitive and vulnerable area known as the mouth, horses will begin learning to receive aids from your hands rather than taking each cue from your body language on the ground.**

Initially, young horses will show signs of being "into pressure," which means they will lean into the pressure they feel rather than moving away to release the pressure. When attaching long-lines, the pressure is considered to be direct pressure (that is, when you want to turn left you apply pressure to the left rein). Horses, being an "into pressure" species, will push (in this case pull) toward the pressure they feel on their mouth or nose so that the pressure increases.

In this instance, toward pressure, for us, is considered an opposite and incorrect request. We want our horses to come off the pressure. Our horses will instinctively turn right when they feel the pressure on the left side of their mouth (to increase the pressure) unless they have been educated to turn left. Once they learn how to release themselves from the pressure by seeking the source, they learn direction as well as slow and stop. It is simple; we just need to know how!

These lessons, in turn, help horses become more comfortable with movement on their backs and around their sides, while gaining confidence and not having to be exposed to the rider at the same time. And unlike the lunge, long-lining will introduce your young horse to the feel of your hands.

Within moments, X learned these vital lessons that were repeated a number of times for him to digest. The lesson was kept informative, short, and interesting, so we could build on it the next day. The most important factor was to teach X something new and yet not overload him in the process. We did just that!

The following day was extremely powerful, as day two always verifies your previous day's work. It's a great gauge to see how much horses retain from their previous experience, which often appears to us as overnight reflection. For the students watching X's five-day demonstration, they witnessed undeniable progress with a young horse learning motivation. The initial "flag" cues, which appeared bold, disappeared in one session and were replaced with light cues that were bordering on invisible.

Within days, X was accompanied by a pony-horse and being ridden in the arena at a walk, trot, and canter, and following my guidance. Each day he learned steps leading up to his successes and long-lining provided him with the tools needed to promote balance, direction, speed control, focus, patience, and more.

The advantages for the seasoned horse are even better

If you have a seasoned horse, never fear. Long-lining has many more advantages for you.

- You can build your horse's muscle tone on both the left and right side, encouraging natural balance and increasing fitness levels while maintaining rhythm. It's a wonderful way to bring your horse back into work after taking time off either for an injury or a vacation.

- For the spooky horse, those lacking confidence and self-esteem, long-lining will help you gain mutual trust and understanding, build focus, patience, and self-control. It will also assist with introducing and exposing your horse to new objects. Try creating your own natural long-lining obstacle course: incorporate trot poles, jumps, or other obstacles, such as the famous yet dreaded tarpaulin.

- For those who are hard to keep occupied/entertained and who need mental stimulus and diversity, you can take this experience out of the round pen and into another environment—like the arena.

- Assess a potentially new horse for you, your client, or friends. You can use this tool to uncover their personalities and discover what motivates them.

- Long-lining is also a perfect exercise to assess your horse's movements under saddle, to look at confirmation and overall physical well-being.

- Aids in communication with equine challenges such as rearing, bolting, balking, or when your horse is barn sour and pushy.

What you need to get started

Equipment Needed:
Think about what you would like to achieve. In its simplest form you really only require a halter and two long lines. You could add a pressure halter, surcingle or roller, saddle (most kinds will do), bridle, and a leather strap. You may also consider placing boots on your horse's legs if you prefer.

Your Safety:

Consider wearing a hard hat on the ground. You may also want to protect your hands from rope burns with gloves. I keep this option open to my students, as I personally don't wear gloves because I like to feel the rope through my fingers. This way I feel more connected to my horse. *However, if you have soft skin, I would highly recommend you wear gloves.*

Your Horse's Safety:

Remember that anything new should be introduced to your horse in a safe environment, such as a round pen. Your horse should feel like the round pen is a place of safety, a place to learn, and also a place to relax. It is a great place to introduce your horse to long-lining techniques.

I have worked in round pens ranging from thirty-five feet to seventy-five feet. I am most comfortable in a fifty-foot round pen and I have found this to be a suitable size for most horses. Most long lines are thirty feet in length and therefore are just the right size for you to be in contact with your horse, while at the same time it is less likely that you will lose them!

No round pen? No problem. You can also set up a small enclosure, sand paddock, grass area, small arena, or a *picadero*. You want it to be small enough for your horse to be safe and not run off with you, but at the same time, not so small that you might cause too much pressure or get kicked.

Also, never forget to ensure that you have the correct footing in an area free of obstructions. Now you are ready to go!

Long-Lining Hints:

- Introduce your horse to his equipment slowly, sensitively, and safely.

- Check your equipment and the fitting.

- Practice on experienced horses first, gradually making your way to young, green horses.

- Practice in a safe environment like a round pen before venturing out in the open.

- Learn how to communicate with your horse through body language, energy, and visualization techniques.

- Practice with human partners to understand your positioning and distance.

- Avoid pulling on the horse's mouth—begin with long-lining off the halter if you are unsure of the horse's reaction or of your own ability.

- Listen to your horse and his needs; always allow for expression.

- Be patient; allow your horse to learn—don't expect perfection from either yourself or your horse the first few sessions.

- Introduce your horse to new objects like an obstacle course and other interesting challenges.

- Establish what motivates your horse and keep the lessons interesting.

- Read your horse; this is an opportunity to gather information about his personality, character, strengths, and weaknesses.

Now that you know a bit about it, I hope you will begin to explore long-lining in your horsemanship. I am convinced that once you really begin using them you will see the benefits that I have discovered and incorporate the often-overlooked art of long-lining into your horsemanship as well.

The Magic Number 3

It is a known fact that if you want to create a bucking horse, then you should fall off your bucking horse three consecutive times. Quite often, horses will learn what to do in a very short period of time. Likewise, they will learn what not to do just as quickly.

Always be aware of the message you are giving your horse. Take time out to reconsider what you are doing and change your plan accordingly. Remember that slow is fast, so you may need to take a step backward in order to move ahead. If your horse is too much for you, seek advice from someone who has more experience than you do.

20

OUR HORSE'S LEARNING STYLES:

EDUCATING EQUINES

"Stop waiting to be ready. Just get started and course-correct as you go. There is no map to greatness Just the willingness to soldier on into the unknown with courage, conviction, and an expectation of Grace."

Cheryl Richardson

www.reachouttohorses.com

Horses at liberty immediately display their true nature, as they are free to make decisions, explore, and express themselves.

Horses go "into" pressure," which means they will seek out what they often have the most fear of, thoroughly examining the nature of that being or object.

I live a double life. I'm not a closet nightclub comedian or a secret government spy, but to some, Natural Horsemanship and Animal Communication are just as far apart. What many don't realize is that they are both very useful tools when it comes to training and working with horses. For me, having both of these in my "tool belt" is a great combination, and many times they complement each other perfectly.

One particularly effective use of these tools is in understanding the different learning styles of individual horses. In my experience, there are twenty-eight characters of horses. Multiply that by the hundreds of different breeds, then add to the mix factors like how each individual was raised and the environment in which he was trained (just to name a few) and you begin to recognize that you have a lifelong discovery ahead of you in determining the true nature of the horse with whom you are working.

Excalibur – Spanish Mustang

Sometimes my skill as a Natural Horsewoman is exactly what I need to understand how best to create the most effective training environment. Take Excalibur, for example:

To better understand where X was coming from, I decided to use a favorite horsemanship tool of mine: the obstacle course. Setting up a simple course in the arena can be a great first step toward exploring your horse's personality, character, and learning styles. Horses at liberty immediately display their true nature, as they are free to make decisions, explore, and express themselves. He only participated once in the obstacle course exercise; he found it intriguing at first, but quickly lost interest during the very first session. X had the good fortune of watching other horses and their people throughout the day. Nickering to all passersby, he watched tentatively, occasionally pawing at the bar to show his interest and willingness to participate.

With a couple of years of handling, hiking, trick and natural horsemanship training under his belt, the obstacles came easily to X. When his turn came, he meandered through the course, touching all the items along the way, occasionally pawing at different items and, at one point, even picking up a tarp with his mouth. Inquisitive, relaxed, confident, and comfortable would describe his mannerisms well.

Over the next thirty minutes X revealed that:

- He learned each task in just one completion. Although many horses learn through repetition, once was all it took for X.

- He learned through observation. Throughout the day, X watched numerous horses explore the arena with excitement, fearlessly approaching and successfully overcoming obstacles. Although he needed to experience the exercise for himself, X witnessed this to be a place of joy by watching the other horses' respective body language and energetic fields. By being situated just a few feet away from the arena, he had one of the best seats in the house.

- He appreciated the time to touch unknown and extraordinary items. Through smell and touch he was able to understand and to digest the information while staying calm and relaxed. Horses have limited depth perception and so the chance to touch and explore texture, depth, sound, and movement is imperative.

- Choice was important to him; X would return to set "stations" either to view them from another angle or gain greater insights. He became more confident, enjoyed performing, and often returned to a number of obstacles that intrigued him. Horses go "into" pressure, which means they will seek out what they often have the most fear of, thoroughly examining the nature of that being or object. Watch when something new enters your horse's pasture and how he will circle it, gradually getting closer and closer...

- Overuse or prolonged exposure in the arena would become boring to him. Variety was paramount to his game. As X lost interest, he would wander off to the edge of the arena seeking grass to nibble. Keeping his interest would prove to be important to maintain a high level of learning.

- Tons of praise influenced his decisions. From capturing the thought and releasing pressure and moments of rest to rubs on the neck and a soothing and encouraging voice, X became motivated by my interaction.

- Witnessing the try, asking vs. telling, and encouraging his creativity enhanced the lesson and solidified the lessons he learned.

Having all the Natural Horsemanship training in the world doesn't necessarily mean you'll be able to solve every problem. This is where the art of Animal Communication can be a lifesaver.

Now under saddle, X and I continue on the journey of discovery; and the lessons in that initial obstacle course still show themselves in all of X's training. Instead of looking for disputes and challenges with a highly intelligent, courageous individual, I have chosen instead to create a training program that takes his individual character, learning style, and needs into account. Each session needs to be a step ahead of X's thoughts while understanding his natural desire to explore.

But having all the Natural Horsemanship training in the world doesn't necessarily mean you'll be able to solve every problem. This is where the art of Animal Communication can be a lifesaver. Through telepathy, another form of communication, I am able to talk directly to the horse. I see in pictures, a little movie or slide show of sorts, with a sense of what is happening, emotions, and the occasional word (spoken and written). It's a language available to all of us if we can just quiet our minds enough to listen.

Bunch of Bills

It is not uncommon for clients to call me with frustrating behavioral issues or learning challenges only to find out, after our communication session, that it was actually a misunderstanding, not a training problem.

This exact situation occurred when I received a call that Oscar, a racehorse, was not doing too well on the track. As I started our session, he began by describing his private home environment. He shared stories about his idyllic upbringing, very friendly family, and his horse/human relations. Oscar gave very specific details of past races he had run and how he felt about the sport itself. He also stated that he opened each race with enthusiasm, staying really close to the rest of the horses, and then he revealed why he would drop back from the pack. It wasn't a training issue, jockey error, or miscalculation. The problem was simply that Oscar just got tired. He didn't have the stamina to continue.

Oscar went on to describe himself physically: size, character, color, and the under-developed muscles in his rear—muscles that are crucial to winning races. This caught my attention and I asked him to share his training regimen with me. Oscar showed me his homemade track. He explained that he did not take a rider, but instead was "ponied" and the speed he gained while he was being led around was by no means sufficient to truly train for a race. Oscar said that "25 mph" was as fast as he could run during the training and no faster. There was no way, in Oscar's mind, that he could win with his current training program.

If you are struggling with a behavioral or learning issue with your horse and you can't seem to solve it with the tools you have, don't just assume the problem is impossible to solve, and don't be afraid to go outside of what is familiar and comfortable to find the answer.

He then showed the specific saddle he carried as well as mentioning a new weight baring one with which he wanted to work. He wanted the training to be intermittent and not consistent and what would help him would be a chance to "breeze" or gallop on the track. That way Oscar could compare his performance to others while gaining the speed and muscle needed. He even

went so far as to mention a place that was a trailer-ride away where they could access a local track and have the opportunity to stay the weekend. He had the heart and desire to win; he just couldn't get his hooves on the right training tools.

What initially had been seen as a possible emotional, mental, or physical stumbling block was simply an oversight in the training program. Oscar came forth with tremendous suggestions to help himself race and win! And without implementing the strength and speed training he needed, no amount of natural horsemanship training (and all the money spent on it) would have made the significant or immediate impact needed to solve the issue.

There's an old saying that "if all you have is a hammer, everything looks like a nail." If you are struggling with a behavioral or learning issue with your horse and you can't seem to solve it with the tools you have, don't just assume the problem is impossible to solve, and don't be afraid to go outside of what is familiar and comfortable to find the answer.

21

"No" to "Go" – Moving from Resistance to Responsiveness

Through communication, connection, and collaboration, we would transform our less-than-effective leadership and eliminate that dreaded feeling of being out-of-control for both horse and human.

---

*Set your pure intentions, making it clear that you wish
to become acquainted with this young being. You have
a picture in your head of how that might look. And yet
your plan is a free-flowing painting, never fixating on
achieving your goal at any cost. Instead, you must
allow this painting to come together naturally
and organically as the partnership evolves.*

It is common when working with our horses, or considering what is best for them and our partnership, to think about it from our human perspective. After all, we are the smarter species. We know what is best. Right?

But if we take a moment to look through our horses' eyes, we will gain a new and intimate perspective, and come to understand a little bit more about the way they see the world and all the sacrifices and contributions they make for us.

The realizations we might uncover could quickly replace the fear and frustration that our ignorance once cultivated with clarity and compassion. Through communication, connection, and collaboration, we would transform our less-than-effective leadership, and eliminate that dreaded feeling of being out-of-control for both horse and human. Exploring and taking ownership of our actions, while experiencing life from our horse's paradigm, would provide space for a "go" instead of a "no."

If you would, just for a moment, take a journey with me. Envision an untouched, untamed, wild foal culled from his mother and his herd of wild mustangs, huddled together with other youngsters, awaiting his fate. His life is no longer his own. He is at the mercy of these aggressive, two-legged creatures.

This is his first encounter with mankind, harsh and terrifying, as he is rounded up, the life he once knew—the only life he knew—running free on his homeland, experiencing mother's tender touch, gone forever. Instead, he is cruelly weaned and incarcerated. He is lonely and afraid. The family that protected him and gave him comfort has been destroyed and will, from this moment on, be nothing more than a distant memory. This was not his choice. It was imposed upon him.

Now imagine that you met this foal and you have the chance to make a difference in his life. You cannot change or eliminate his traumatic ordeal, nor can you return him to his homeland. But you can be a part of his future. You can create a new impression, one that puts him solidly on a new, positive path. Your interactions could pave the way for his future. You have only one chance at a first impression and you want it to be the right one.

For that to happen you must:

Begin to learn and speak *his language*, the silent and secret language of Equus. It includes familiarizing yourself with his culture as well as moving in a manner he understands. Move as if you are traveling through molasses, recognizing the minute gestures with which he has learned to communicate. These gestures are invisible to almost all. They require a keen eye to be noticed: the look in the eye, a subtle shift in weight distribution, the slightest of movements, actions, which "ask" and "thank," movements that open up and create a dialogue.

Organize and formulate your thoughts. When you enter his environment, you are focused on only one thing: this little being. Grounding yourself allows the stresses of your day to dissolve. You must put your fears and concerns aside to be able to hold a positive attitude. The space you share is nothing less than *sacred.*

Set your pure intentions, making it clear that you wish to become acquainted with this young being. You have a picture in your head of how that might look. And yet your plan is a free-flowing painting, never fixating on achieving your goal at any cost. Instead, you must allow this painting to come together naturally and organically as the partnership evolves.

Remain in the "now" and the "not-to-distant" future, all the while embracing your strengths as you show up for your horse. And you remind yourself to be open to all that may come. Your mind remains open, as you are able to watch for all that your horse "offers" and, in turn, acknowledge his tries, no matter how small, celebrating every success!

Realize that your horse has a way to show his intentions as well. You must capture his whisper. You both share this ability to read one another's eyes.

Learn to recognize his nuances and adapt your responses to a more "natural" and organic approach. His intention is reflected in his eye before any movement is seen.

We must replace force, dominance, and compliance with compassion, communication, and collaboration.

Be it a . . .

- Twinkle in the eye
- Sight of sadness or sorrow
- Recognition, response, or relaxation
- Disconnection through to a dialogue
- Flash of fear or fight
- Look of compliance or control
- Heartfelt connection

Learn to recognize his nuances and adapt your responses to a more "natural" and organic approach. His intention is reflected in his eye before any movement is seen.

Move from "doing to your horse" into a deeper philosophy of practicing, playing "with your horse." Encourage his individual character. Let his personality develop and shine through. Where many discourage horses to reach their full potential, you must see the value to encourage your horse as you realize your dreams together, in partnership.

Discover the favorite scratching spots on his body that he is unable to reach. No longer task-oriented, dominance takes a back seat. Instead, driven by exploration, expansion, creativity, and collaboration, you seek that which encourages him forward and builds on his success. Your interactive engagement guides your initial daily activities and responsibilities. Your horse is given a voice and a choice while you create the fundamentals for him to find the "right" way forward.

Recognize his learning style, the length of lesson he appreciates to be able to process and retain the information provided. You must see the sensitivity he possesses and praise him in the manner he understands and embraces. Crowned with creativity, your sessions need to carry an abundance of variety, adjusting the time you may need to repeat aspects of your repertoire for mutual understanding.Navigating through becomes a normal way of being instead of putting your will onto him.

Where we may anticipate and understand the overall outcome, and realize where our intentions and our actions lead, our horse does not. As we introduce these young and innocent beings to their first human touch, grooming session, halter, leading, syringe, blanket, picking up feet, farrier preparation, vet visit, and trailer-loading experiences, we must remember it is always their first time. We only have one chance to make a first and everlasting impression, and we want to make it a good one.

We must ask ourselves if we are truly willing to take them unconditionally into our folds, and promise to honor and protect them, to serve and support them, to heal and guide them, and be the true stewards we are supposed to be.

As far as we know, they may resist and be completely perplexed as to why their heads are restricted, why they no longer have the freedom of their head carriage and movement, and why they have been deprived of their liberty. The very aspects they have held on to in their short lives and not only loved, but also never known any differently, are gone forever. It is likely they were taught to protect their heads from all handling by their elders, or were driven by fear to hide, disassociate, do their best to run away, and, if unable to do so, to fight for their lives.

You can see how easily individuals who do not understand what is happening can slip into abusing these confused and frightened foals. Many have been roped, choked, laid down, placed into chutes, forced to endure children's rodeos, starved, neglected, bred as by-products of the industry, left in feedlots, and even intercepted on their way to slaughter. If we don't hear them, who will?

Although this story is about the foals and other wild horses that I have encountered in my twenty-plus years of training, it really is the story of all the horses we touch and influence. We must ask ourselves if we are truly willing to take them unconditionally into our folds, and promise to honor and protect them, to serve and support them, to heal and guide them, and be the true stewards we are supposed to be.

It is our duty to introduce these untouched and occasionally unblemished individuals into our world with kindness. No matter how young or old, unhandled or over-handled, innocent or wise, no horse needs to be treated with callous convenience, as simply . . . a horse. Each has his or her individual perspective and life's purpose. We owe it to our horses to take their individuality into account.

It is, without a doubt, the more difficult journey and the road less travelled. It can be frustratingly more challenging than simply demanding that they meet us where we are or forcing them to abide by a systemized approach. But if we insist, they try and bring their best to us, then we must do the same for them. We must replace force, dominance, and compliance with compassion, communication, and collaboration.

Remember, none of us get up in the morning and set out to make our horses' and our own lives miserable. We do not consciously seek to hurt or be hurt, endanger or dominate, or strive to live a life of stress. We do not create plans to make our days more complicated than they need to be. We all wish to enjoy our experiences with our equine companions . . . together. And to do that we need to remember to laugh, live, appreciate, and respect life.

Simply put, it is a call to listen, to connect with your heart, allowing your horse to be the individual he was meant to be, and receive the gift of the "go."

22

Free School Your Way to Whoa!

THE PAST IS *your Lesson*
THE PRESENT IS *your Gift*
THE FUTURE IS *your Motivation*

PHOTO: MAYA HORSEY

REACHOUTTOHORSES.COM

Liberty work is a time when you and your horse are truly on equal terms, when he can speak his mind and you both get to experience the joy of freedom from tack, equipment, and lines.

As with any tool, the effectiveness or abuse is not in the tool itself but in the hands of those who use it.

A good *whoa* is one of the most important things you can teach your horse. Doing so at liberty can help strengthen your communication skills.

Whoa there! For centuries, horsemanship seemed to be all about man dictating to the horse. Good horsemanship was demonstrated by how well you could train your horse, regardless of the methods you used or the negative effects they had on the animal.

Thankfully, times have changed and horsemanship has evolved into something much kinder and far more effective. At Reach Out to Horses, we are committed to not only training horses but to creating a trust-based partnership with them, giving them a voice, and instead of "breaking" them, allowing their true personalities to shine through, creating a genuine bond built on communication and respect.

Communicate freely

Nowhere is this partnership more obvious than when you're working with your horse at liberty. Liberty work can be very fulfilling and a lot of fun. It's a time when you and your horse are truly on equal terms, when he can speak his mind and you both get to experience the joy of freedom from tack, equipment, and lines. It's a chance to explore one another while combining educational exercises into the mix.

I've heard others utilize the word "Ho," but I caution against this because it sounds similar to "No" and you might accidently create an unwanted stop when you least expect it!

The round pen can be a great place to work with your horse at liberty. Still, many misconceptions exist about the round pen. Some people love it, some hate it, some use it, and some don't. As with any tool, the effectiveness or abuse is not in the tool itself but in the hands of those who use it. I use the round pen for the "reaching out" process, to create a specific contract with my horses, and for free schooling.

Free schooling allows you to choreograph your lesson, going with the flow and feeling what your horse has to offer. As long as your horse appreciates his environment and is enthusiastic and willing, free schooling can be built into your weekly activities.

Free schooling is an ideal tool for removing excess energy, rehabilitating, building muscle and endurance, "playing" with your horse, teaching "trick training," viewing his movement, introducing voice commands, and more.

Whoa there!

If you have thought about connecting on this level, but didn't quite know how, here's a great place to start. Try using free schooling to introduce your horse to the importance of the word whoa. This exercise will enhance your connection and communication and empower both you and your horse. Incidentally, I've heard others utilize the word "Ho," but I caution against this because it sounds similar to "No" and you might accidently create an unwanted stop when you least expect it!

Teaching *whoa* step-by-step

1. Begin driving your horse around the round pen, remaining in the "driving zone" about 45 degrees behind the barrel of your horse. I will sometimes bring a line in with me for safety and to enhance my communication. Always remember: there is a difference between driving and chasing, and your intention should never be to create fear in your horse.

2. Decide on the exact location within the round pen where you would like your horse to stop.

3. Say "*whoa*" before you take any action to stop him.

4. Keep your eyes on your horse's eyes and step with determination into his path of travel; do this well ahead of him to allow him to understand and see your request.

5. Gauge the distance needed to be effective. Do not walk directly toward your horse's eye and head, as that will turn him.

6. Do not get too close to the horse or "pinch" him against the round pen wall. It may cause him to bolt or even kick out.

7. Gauge the correct amount of energy needed to facilitate the stop—project or absorb your energy where needed.

8. If your horse is traveling in a clockwise direction, use your right hand to influence his nose; use your left hand to influence his nose if he's moving counterclockwise.

Always remember: there is a difference between driving and chasing, and your intention should never be to create fear in your horse.

---

9.   Step toward your horse, if needed, to prevent him rom turning toward you.

10. Keep your horse's nose straight in front of him to ask for a stop on the round pen wall (you can build up to this).

11. Use your line to back up your hand gesture, if needed.

12. Look directly at his hips if he is about to swing them toward you.

13. Plant your feet firmly when you know your horse will come to a stop.

14. Soften your posture slightly at the moment he stops, as a reward.

15. Maintain your positioning.

16. Hold your horse in this position, increasing the duration over time.

17. Return to the driving position and say, "Walk on".

18. Repeat multiple times, gradually eliminating bold body language and becoming more subtle until you eventually remove the body language altogether and replace it solely with the verbal cue.

19. Always end on a positive note and do not spend more time in the round pen than your horse can handle. The round pen should be a place of learning and fun, not work and fear.

The steps themselves are really quite simple. However, the true art of free schooling is not a step-by-step process but rather lies in your ability to understand and communicate with your horse. After all, you cannot give him a voice and discover what he has to offer if you can't understand what he is saying.

The best part is that this doesn't just apply to teaching your horse to stop. It can open many doors. You can take this exercise to so many levels, from the ground through to horseback. You are limited only by your imagination. Just remember—success is in the listening, not the speaking. Happy trails!

— Photo Diary —

Alexa, a beautiful Quarter Horse mare, attended the ROTH Holistic Horsemanship Foundation class for the day. Completely open to what would take place, I entered the round pen to be greeted by Alexa, whose soft approach, sensitivity, and kindness immediately touched my heart and everyone's watching. We spent some time, sharing space together, blending energy, and creating a close connection. The conversation began the moment we were within view of one another.

When it was time to engage in learning "whoa," I made a few initial changes to my body language. By raising my shoulders from a passive position, I asked Alexa to pay attention. Standing square in front of her, I created a boundary and maintained the space between us by projecting a "bubble of energy" and asking her to keep the distance. I looked her directly in the eyes, telling her I wished her to stand back, and reinforced my energy bubble while watching her response. I regularly use these subtle nuances in both body language and energy to effectively communicate with my horses.

In order to gain a stop, you have to have forward motion. Driving Alexa forward while I was behind her barrel at a 45-degree angle, and using my body language, I communicated to her to move out. My eyes watched her eyes closely to read her mood and upcoming actions, while my shoulders were parallel, or square, to her shoulders. My heart space was facing her heart space (located behind her shoulder), and directing energy like an invisible laser beam. My hips/pelvis faced her shoulder while we maintained forward motion. As she asked to rejoin me, I communicated to her with a hand gesture, asking her to continue moving forward and concentrate on keeping the flow. My open left hand redirected her nose forward.

Correct body positioning, shoulder placement, head carriage, and eye contact are crucial to helping guide your horse with clarity.

You cannot give your horse a voice and discover what he has to offer if you can't understand what he is saying.

Clear intention is key when asking your horse to stop. Plan where you want the horse to stop in the round pen, and be aware as to why you chose that location. Always stay away from the gate as this will eventually act as a magnet to which your horse will gravitate vs. learning how to stop from your physical and verbal cues. It is good to repeat the "stop" in the same location multiple times prior to changing direction.

Alexa really appreciated praise and was rewarded throughout the session with a release of pressure for each "try" she made. Her "tries" included: forward motion, softening and relaxation, and of course stopping on command. Each try would be rewarded by the most suitable gesture of thought, relaxed eyes, slower pace, soft shoulders, and lowered hands or arms. But the most appreciated reward for Alexa was connecting with me in the center of the round pen where we spent time bonding. We repeated our lesson a number of times, which lasted no more than ten to fifteen minutes and finished on a superb note. It was clear that Alexa enjoyed her time together remaining sensitive and motivated.

23

REACH OUT TO THE REMEDIAL HORSE

REACHOUTTOHORSES.COM

"UNTIL WE MAKE THE UNCONSCIOUS CONSCIOUS IT WILL DIRECT OUR LIVES AND WE'LL CALL IT FATE."

JUNG

"Imagine, your feet are your most valuable tool of defense, and now you are told to give up your defense and pick up your feet when asked."

I am often asked to help people with the horse they just can't handle. They've tried everything and their horse just will not stop the behavior and, in some cases, drastic action will be taken if they or someone else can't "fix" the problem.

To begin addressing these issues I always steer my clients toward the behavior of the wild horse. Horses have survived through history using instinct, adaptation, and an effective non-verbal language that goes well beyond the unspoken. When observing horses in a natural habitat you will find them running, bucking, rearing, kicking, and biting one another out of play. You will witness their curious, gregarious nature, along with their social interaction. You will not see them stall-walking, weaving, or wind-sucking!

It is crucial to remember that, so often, these majestic creatures are taken out of their natural environment and placed in a completely unfamiliar world. We force them to go against their natural instincts and behavior patterns, without giving it a second thought. Take a moment to imagine yourself to be a free-roaming horse.

Horses' Natural Behavior	Human Demands
You are used to roaming several miles a day.	…now you become confined in a 12x12 stall.
You normally graze 16–18 hours a day as a trickle-feeder.	…now you are on a scheduled feeding regime.
Your feet are your most valuable tool of defense.	…now you are told to give up your defense and pick up your feet.
You are sociable and love interaction and mutual grooming.	…now you are too valuable to be turned out with others.
You have learnt to protect yourself by fleeing. If you cannot flee you fight. You may kick or bite or buck.	…now you are introduced to your first saddle and when you try to deter the "predator" by bucking you get reprimanded!

These are but a few changes we make to horses' daily lives and a few expectations we place on them. Horses' instincts have been honed over the 54 million years they have inhabited this planet and the relatively short period of time they have lived in domestication is certainly not enough to change the natural behaviors and instincts that have served them for so long.

Many times, in fact, these natural behaviors can be seen in the "problems" of domesticated horses. Cribbing, for example, can be classed as a form of grazing. A cribbing horse may be lacking jaw movement and exercise, and because of that may start to chew other parts of its surroundings. The horse that "stall walks" or "weaves" is exercising its natural instinct to steadily forage. Understanding the natural behaviors and survival instincts will help you to better approach your horse's "problems" and "vices."

As horse trainers, riders, managers, and horse lovers it is always our responsibility to investigate all possibilities. If you are working with someone else's horse it is obviously useful to know the history from the owners. But you should then place that information in the back of your mind.

It is far more important to read what the horse is telling you about its own history. People perceive events in different ways, both from other people and especially from horses. Hence, although the history of the horse may explain some of the behaviors you observe, it is only the horse itself that can tell you the true story.

One owner I worked with told me the story of her young paint colt. She explained that she and her husband would often go on trail rides and when they would come upon a stream her colt would head right over and begin to lie down. He would literally immerse himself in the water. She didn't believe that it was his playful nature; instead, she was quite distraught about the situation and wanted it solved. I determined that he was young and had some handling and training. There was no mention of any accidents that may have occurred and, most importantly, no past or present injuries.

"Imagine that you are sociable and love interaction and mutual grooming with others. Now you are too valuable to be turned out with others."

"Horses' instincts have been honed over the 54 million years that they have inhabited this planet, and the relatively short period of time they have lived in domestication is certainly not enough to change the natural behaviors and instincts that have served them for so long."

Next, I needed to assess the horse's physical wellbeing to see if the root cause may lie in injury or pain. With all "problems" such as these we need to consider all possibilities including:

an inexperienced rider
low workload vs. high energy
an incorrect feeding schedule
back pain
an ill-fitting saddle

dentistry needs
heat cycles and hormones
the experience of an abusive rider

These problems can usually be addressed by using equine chiropractors, tack fitters, nutritionists, and other equine specialists.

I conducted a round-pen session with this young colt using the Reach Out to Horses® methods. To begin with he was reluctant to take the head-collar and a little head-shy. During the procedure, it became apparent that he had pain in his head, neck, withers, and back area. He also informed me through his language, motion, and energy that he was very sore throughout his entire body.

As I was sharing what this young colt was expressing openly and loudly, the clients began to tell me that, in fact, when saddling him a year prior with a Western Saddle, he had flipped over and landed on his back. After the incident, they continued to ride him intermittently. This explained why he was seeking to lie down in the cold water—he was trying to relieve his discomfort. This young colt was particularly forgiving. He tolerated a high degree of discomfort and was "shouting" to his people to take notice. I was happy to finally be able to get his message across to the owner and through conventional and alternative healing methods his issues would easily be resolved.

Once the pain is alleviated and your horse has regained his confidence, he will gain a new understanding and stop associating saddles and riders to pain. He will begin to view them as allies to be trusted. In listening to the horse and trying to understand his motives you may find the answer to the problem surprisingly simple.

"Although the history of the horse may explain some of the behaviors you observe, it is only the horse himself who can tell you the true story."

"In listening to the horse and trying to understand his motives you may find the answer to the problem surprisingly simple."

Here are some questions you can use as guidelines to help you with some of the issues you may be having:

1. When/where did the change in behavior begin?
2. How did the behavior manifest?
3. Who is responsible for this problem?
4. Why was this problem created?
5. What are we going to do to change it?

Reaching out to your horse will restore trust and confidence in humans. It is the foundation to all communication and can take on many forms. "Reach Out" will allow you to learn to read and communicate with your horse while building a trust-based relationship. It is the beginning to all success and will aid in improving existing relationships, embarking on new partnerships, and assessing character and health.

Listen Up!

Your horse's ears let you know where he's receiving his information. In a schooling environment where your horse is either at liberty or on a single line, his inside ear will be rotated toward you in what I call a "locked-on-to-me" position. I would recommend that you see this at least 75 percent of the time or more; ideally you are looking for 100 percent. This tells you that your horse is paying attention to you and listening to what you have to say. The outside ear will focus on motion and sounds from outside the round pen/arena/paddock or picadero.

The ears will also reflect emotions or how a horse is feeling at any time. If his ears are flat back, he has become aggressive; if they are perked forward, he is paying attention or alert to something in front. When saddling a young horse, he will have his ears facing toward the saddle, not because he is upset or mean, but because he is taking in information from the rear. Horses often display "floppy" ears when they are uncertain or confused.

24

TOP TEN BODY-LANGUAGE POSTURES

What we can learn from horses is infinitely more valuable than what we can teach them

ReachOutToHorses.com

The horse's language is predominantly silent, and body language and gestures are a big part of that communication. Learning any language takes time, commitment, patience, and practice.

Awareness ranks high on the horse's list of survival traits and is especially displayed in herd leaders.

Observing our horses can bring great pleasure and peace, but if we're paying attention, it can also help us to gain an immense understanding of their nature. The horse's language is predominantly silent, and body language and gestures are a big part of that communication.

Learning any language takes time, commitment, patience, and practice. Sometimes it's helpful to have an interpreter too. Here are ten of the most common body-language gestures and postures you will encounter in your horse.

1. Awareness

Awareness ranks high on the horse's list of survival traits and is especially displayed in herd leaders. With their high head carriage, horses focus on distant objects. Their ears pinpoint the location of their focus as well as reveal their mood. As flight animals, horses are reactive and a chain effect can occur within the herd. When in an overall relaxed state, "floppy" ears to the side show contentment; when at work, this same gesture can denote confusion. When creating a team of two, you want your horse to pay attention to you, with his ears pointed toward you.

2. Move

Stallions often use "snaking"—lowering their heads and pinning their ears flat back against their necks in order to move not only the herd but also unwanted strangers from the area. Some are more demonstrative than others, but either way this motion means "move" in no uncertain terms. You will know when this gesture is meant for you as your horse will stare you in the eyes, square his shoulders toward you, and pin his ears flat back. The intimidating energy is also very clear!

3. Listening/Focus

Ears signal what horses are listening to and where their attention lies. When placed forward, horses are focused on something ahead. When positioned softly backward, they are paying attention to something from the rear. Each ear works independently and follows movement. Wherever your horse places his ear, his eye will follow.

4. Play

As social creatures, horses love to play. Their movements are intentional and although they sometimes appear rough they usually involve mutual consent. You can capture the "whisper" in your horse's eye and, with practice, determine a soft, playful eye versus a skeptical, concerned, fearful, or dangerous one. Horses play both horse-to-horse and horse-to-human. Their mouths will remain supple—especially apparent in an extended top lip!

5. Mutual Grooming

Mutual grooming is an important part of herd interaction. It's a sign of mutual trust and respect. For me, it's always a compliment when our horses invite us to become one with the herd. Their eyes remain soft, the head curves around your body, and they nuzzle you with their upper lips. Sometimes forgetting their strength, they use their teeth and have to be reminded to be gentle with our delicate skin, and nuzzle only.

6. Licking and Chewing

Licking and chewing is a sign of relaxation, understanding a request, and either a release of pressure or emotion. This communication is known to mean: "I am an herbivore and mean no harm." A tight jaw on the other hand would denote fear and concern.

7. Curiosity

Naturally curious, horses enjoy investigating and engaging with unusual objects and beings. As they explore, you will often notice their ears forward, neck carriage reaching toward the object, a focused eye, soft muzzle, and large, exploring nostrils.

8. Flehmen Response

Stallions often check piles of manure for identification and marking purposes. The flehmen response, fondly known to many as "smiling," is actually a horse's response to an unusual smell. In order to identify the smell, the scent travels from the upper lip into the nose to the Jacob's organ.

An instantaneous tightening and tucking of the hind-end muscles, an extremely high head carriage and a concerned eye are all indications that your horse is about to flee. If you take away flight, you often induce fight or freeze responses.

Capturing your horse's initial thought can often eliminate misunderstandings, prevent undesirable behavior patterns, and enhance your relationship

*When we understand the herd guidelines to which
our horses adhere, and that they are sentient beings
and talk to us through non-verbal communication,
a whole new world opens up before our eyes.*

9. Worry

Worry in horses can be identified when their tails rise—particularly seen in many demonstrative hot-blooded horses such as Arabians. Head carriage high, they show the whites of their eyes and are light on their feet.

10. Flight Mode

An instantaneous tightening and tucking of the hind-end muscles; an extremely high head carriage and a concerned eye are all indications that your horse is about to flee. If you take away flight, you often induce fight or freeze responses.

Better Communication Makes for Better Relationships

Horses are often subtle with their body language, but those "whispers" can quickly escalate to "shouts" if the conversation goes unheard. Capturing your horse's initial thought can often eliminate misunderstandings, prevent undesirable behavior patterns, and enhance your relationship. Domesticated horses are asked to adapt to our lifestyles, which in many instances goes directly against their natural instincts. Many times, their messages can appear similar and are often misinterpreted.

Before you expect and demand your horse to adjust to an unnatural world, you can enhance your relationship with him if you first reach out and meet him by learning the intricacies and subtleties of his body language. When we understand the herd guidelines to which our horses adhere, and that they are sentient beings and talk to us through non-verbal communication, a whole new world opens up before our eyes.

25

TOBI, THE ONE-EYED HORSE

Saving one horse may not change the World But surely it will Change the World for that One Horse

ReachOuttoHorses.com

Horse whispering, for me, is the ability to capture the whisper of the horse, which is known to begin with a thought, and this thought is often captured within a glimpse of their eye. **Our horses are known to predominantly converse through their movements, but if we acknowledge their initial communication to be intention, thoughts, and energy, much happens that goes unseen.**

Train yourself to feel the subtleties of the energy moving between you, allowing yourself to tune-in to this often untapped, intuitive art. **Through the energy, you will know not only your horse's emotional state but often her intentions too.**

Be conscious of your thoughts. Horses see in pictures and the images you hold are easily picked up by them. Visualize what you are about to do, thereby showing her in unspoken words what she can come to expect. Your visualization will, in turn, be reflected in your movements providing confidence and clarity.

Read your horse's actions, from the minutest motion, so that you are conscious of her needs. Allow Tobi to understand that you are capable of protecting her. As all horses do, she seeks a true leader, one who shows extreme awareness of her surroundings so that she may completely trust and feel comfortable.

Be mindful that Tobi may be protective of the area where the eye was doctored, and if this was the case, behavioral challenges can creep in if not handled correctly (such as head-shyness and biting). Some jumpiness can appear if taken by surprise and *vocal communication will be imperative.*

In my experience, the right environment has a lot to do with how the horse adapts to his new state of being. Horses who have evolved into mature personalities may remain grounded and little difference will be apparent. However, you may find that some spookiness appears and, in that case, during training, repetition can be another answer as you realize that the nature of the horse includes flight to be the primary form of defense. In the case of blind horses, these lessons are often not overcome because their primary instinct has to remain intact and it would not matter how often the lesson be repeated as it's not fair or possible to instill.

Specifically acknowledging an individual's needs is paramount and, as such, if there is a likelihood of concern and upset in a new environment, one would be particularly diligent in keeping stress levels to the minimum. Taking the living conditions, training environment, and social network into consideration will alleviate many undesired eventualities and keep all in balance. **Remaining compassionate instead of driving these areas home for personal gain will be repaid in volumes.** Consider including another respected and reliable horse as support for any given training experience.

Thinking in Pictures

Horses are associative thinkers. They see in pictures and relate certain images to specific events. For the bad events, it's up to you to change the picture with a new and improved version! If your horse has been spooked out on a ride in a particular location, for example, she will remember this. She will associate the rain jacket flapping on the back of the saddle during a windy day with the location of the event—that is, right where the woods began. If you don't deal with this frightening situation, this memory will be waiting to terrorize your horse for the next ride at this location.

It is crucial that you take the time to change the image for a better one. Be consistent and patient, without fear or force and you'll find your friend can relax and digest the new information.

Use visualization techniques—visualizing not only helps you see how you want a situation to develop, but it can also positively affect your body language. Taking it another step further, we can communicate with our horses through sending and receiving pictures. Why not show them through your mind what you are working toward achieving?

26

NATURALLY CLAUSTROPHOBIC

REACHOUTTOHORSES.COM

It takes courage to grow up and be what you are destined to become.

Δll horses, by nature, are claustrophobic to some degree. Understanding why your equine partner reacts this way will help you develop a program to make him feel more comfortable in tight situations.

> *It's important that we take the whole horse into consideration, including his breed, personality, environment, history, and handling. To understand our horse's needs, we must first understand him.*

How and when claustrophobia may show itself

- Pulling back on halters during leading, ponying, or when tied

- Entering narrow spaces, stalls, barns, enclosures, and trailers

- Unprovoked flying back out of a trailer, chute, stands, or other restrictive spaces

- Freezing, bracing, and rigid responses when restrained

Because they've evolved to be free-roaming beings, most horses have claustrophobic tendencies. But some display it more than others. At times, it can be difficult to determine what's happening with a particular horse—whether it's a phobia or behavioral issue. If you know what you are looking at though, certain situations will highlight the horse's reaction and give you very specific insights into which it could be.

It's important that we take the whole horse into consideration, including his breed, personality, environment, history, and handling. To understand our horse's needs, we must first understand him.

Teaching to Give to Pressure

More than a decade ago, I was training a horse to load during a natural horsemanship clinic at Monty Roberts' Flag Is Up Farms in California.

I didn't know my equine partner intimately, so I began our session first in the round pen, to gain a connection, and then with some halter work. We used the Dually halter, which is one I still use today. It is a very effective pressure halter specifically designed to teach horses to come off pressure.

Horses are innately an "into pressure" species. It is a well-known fact that you have to teach them not to lean into pressure, but instead, to "come off pressure" by moving away from it. With a little coaxing and correct timing, they learn very quickly to move out of discomfort and into comfort.

My methods include unloading horses once they have offered to load, thereby giving them instant rewards through the release of pressure within the trailer itself, and the freedom to walk away.

A trailer is an enclosed space and allowing the horse to exit, breathe, and reenter multiple times is empowering for him.

Listen to the Horse

I began the loading lesson by showing my horse the entrance to the trailer. Our style of training includes leading the horse into the trailer; if he has trouble entering, you remain in the trailer, asking him to step forward toward you. It can be an extremely effective method, but precision of body language, posture, feel, and timing are crucial. Given the voice and the opportunity, the horse I was working with eventually began to load, albeit reluctantly.

My methods include unloading horses once they have offered to load, thereby giving them instant rewards through the release of pressure within the trailer itself, and the freedom to walk away. Pressure is not only created through direct manipulation of the halter, but also through situations, environments, and locations. A trailer is an enclosed space and allowing the horse to exit, breathe, and reenter multiple times is empowering for him.

It took approximately thirty minutes to load the first time. During that time, every "try" had been rewarded in multiple ways. A second and then a third lesson followed this, each taking approximately twenty minutes.

Common "non-loaders" will typically improve dramatically, loading with rhythm and ease, constantly building on their previous experiences to the point of eventually loading themselves. This, however, was not the case on that particular day. This horse voiced his concerns without extreme panic. He would load, but remained "sticky" and resistant, trying to share his story in the only way he knew how—through his actions.

So I voiced my thoughts. "This horse is trying his best," I said, "but something doesn't add up."

My student finally revealed a key piece of the puzzle. "We drove here from Arizona," she stated. "The temperatures were soaring. The butt bar burned his rear on the way here—those are the marks you can see."

It had not dawned on my student to share this crucial piece of information prior to the lesson. How precious this horse was for putting up with our training session and expressing his fear the way he did! It was just another example of how forgiving horses can be, and a great lesson in recognizing equine behavior. Although known to be naturally claustrophobic, this horse was not displaying claustrophobic tendencies— he was simply telling his own story.

Sometimes all that's needed to change a horse's life is creativity and patience.

Leila, on the other hand, was a completely different situation. During the Reach Out to Horses Holistic Horsemanship Certification Course one summer, this Spanish Mustang's guardian expressed concerns about her horse entering shelters, arenas, and trailers. Despite years of habituation and good handling, Leila was exhibiting classic signs of claustrophobia and there had been little improvement.

We prepared Leila with a week of Reach Out methodology, which included round penning, T.L.C. halter work, in-hand obstacle course work, spook busting, ground driving, and loading experiences.

We also supported her specifically through her intense fear of enclosures during the behavioral modification day of the course. I set up a three-paneled round-pen stall in the indoor arena with the fourth panel acting as a potential gate if all went well. I knew Leila was familiar with these particular panels, as we had restarted her under saddle in the very same environment the previous year. I then began to instruct students to lead her in and out on a loose line, giving her plenty of room for expression.

Maintaining pure intention, clear focus, and soft guidance, Leila accepted her task quite naturally. We incorporated praise, and she expressed her recognition and appreciation of this praise throughout the entire experience.

Past Problems

In my experience, if there is little-to-no improvement during a training session, and a potentially violent outbreak from the horse is still possible, it's worth considering his past. It may have included abuse, PTSD, or claustrophobic tendencies. In such cases, it's advisable to go slow and build in a particularly compassionate and alternative approach.

The stimulus was gradually strengthened with added parachutes to the sides of the panels, thereby removing Leila's vision and slowly enclosing her. With clarity and consistency, she continued to accept our requests. The roof was added in stages and the gate closed once she was ready. It proved to be a highly successful training session.

As simple as it may sound, this single session helped Leila comfortably frequent her outside shelter. And the lesson stayed with her as she loaded into the trailer to go home! Sometimes all that's needed to change a horse's life is creativity and patience.

27

RIDING FROM THE GROUND

Long-lining has many benefits, including increased communication, trust, confidence, and training

The horse knows who you are often before you do.
– Anna Twinney

REACHOUTTOHORSES.COM

The combination of body language and lines allows your conversation to flow naturally, in a language your horse already knows, as you communicate nonverbally with her while simultaneously influencing both lines.

The safest place to introduce double lines to your horse is in the round pen!

Long-lining is an extremely powerful tool. Often referred to as ground-driving or "riding from the ground," it bridges the gap between foundational groundwork and riding. It's also invaluable for helping your horse reach her full potential in a safe and effective manner. By incorporating this practice into your horse's training, you can gain a better feel and connection with her. It can also:

- Teach your horse (and probably yourself) the significance of proximity, positioning, and intricate movements

- Develop, strengthen, and clarify the communication between you and your horse

- Bridge the gap between your non-verbal conversation (body language and physical cues) and your communication in the saddle

- Create a confident, well-rounded, balanced horse (both physically and mentally)

- Safely introduce your horse to cues from the halter or bit (if you choose to use one)

Creativity is key as you explore your horse's capabilities with turns, circles, serpentines, transitions, and, for the adventurous, flying changes!

Ground-driving is an art that spans colt-starting all the way to working with top performance horses. Unquestionably, it requires a lot of time to learn the intricacies.

The combination of body language and lines allows your conversation to flow naturally, in a language your horse already knows, as you communicate nonverbally with her while simultaneously influencing both lines. And the best part is that long-lining is useful regardless of where your horse is in her life or career.

This is also your opportunity to be creative and add some fun and partnership into your horse's training. You can create your course specifically for your circumstances, choreograph each lesson, and incorporate your horse's needs, desires, learning style, and more into it. The options are virtually limitless; ground-driving has something to offer everyone, regardless of weather, environment, or time constraints!

Step 1: Ground-driving in the round pen

The safest place to introduce double lines to your horse is in the round pen! Take the time to get to know her capabilities, understanding, and knowledge of this exercise or, if she is new to long-lines, teach her the complete process—from accepting the lines through to understanding the communication of the line aids. With the correct use of the lines, you can both desensitize your horse to alarming motions, or sensitize her to listening and coming off the pressure.

The inside line acts as the inside leg and can both influence forward motion as well as a yield to the outside. The outside line will focus on creating stimulus from behind to engage the hindquarters. The outside line influences speed as it does when taken into work under saddle. Soft hands will either introduce or reinforce direction to the left and right as well as speed control for downward transitions, stops, and backing up.

Working in the round pen will create an environment for your horse to understand all the cues that will later be taken into work under saddle. Creativity is key as you explore your horse's capabilities with turns, circles, serpentines, transitions, and, for the adventurous, flying changes!

Step 2: Ground-driving in the arena

Out of the round pen and into the arena! As you remove the confining boundaries of the round pen, your horse will begin to seek and explore, and can be easily distracted. For safety's sake, first teach her to circle on a 50-foot circle without the walls of the round pen for support. This movement can easily be turned into the "one-rein stop" if you need it. Once a round circle has been achieved in both directions, and preferably at both a walk and trot, it's time to expand to the whole arena.

The arena is your classroom. Be creative and work from the ground just as you would in the saddle.

For example, you can incorporate:

- Forward motion
- Straight lines
- Half halts
- Transitions
- Turns
- Stops
- Circles
- Serpentines
- Side-passes
- Pole work
- Obstacles
- Anything else you think is needed!

In our Reach Out to Horses® classes, the obstacle courses are invaluable. From utilizing the courses at liberty, through in-hand leading, ground-driving, and right up into the saddle, they have become places of higher learning. In Step 2, you can teach your horse a whole array of movements to build confidence, creativity, and condition.

Step 3: Ground-driving in nature

A common training exercise in England and Europe involves long-lining young horses away from the confined spaces of the round pen and arena. Done on paths, tracks, roads, and through villages, it can be some of the best preparation for the horse before starting work under saddle.

Many horses will benefit from exploring the outdoors and being away from home. You will also challenge your skills and build on the trust between you and your horse as she leaves her herd and ventures into an unknown environment with you. This is the moment in which you must step up as leader of your herd of two.

If you are unsure, the safest way to ground-drive in the open is to have a companion walk alongside your horse, just as in the arena. Everything changes when exploring new territories *so expect the unexpected.* Remember to keep it easy for you and your horse. If you are both having fun, the learning happens naturally!

Ground-driving is an art that spans colt-starting all the way to working with top performance horses. Unquestionably, it requires a lot of time to learn the intricacies. However, once you master this often-misunderstood skill, you will never want to be without it because you'll experience perfect feel, timing, and balance, and gain trust, respect, leadership, and focus from your horse. It will enhance your training, fill in many holes, and give you a safe and effective way to translate your foundational groundwork right into the saddle.

Troubleshooting

If you get into trouble and your horse begins to pull or ignore the line cues, circle her to regain your composure and influence her feet. If you feel like you are losing "control" or becoming too hard on your horse's head, you can always ask a handler to support you.

Have the handler clip onto the halter with a 14-foot rope and walk next to your horse to provide clarity. The additional person provides guidance at a slight distance and can be a calming influence on the situation. He or she is not there to lead, but to listen to both the horse and trainer, and guide from behind when needed.

Tools for ground-driving

1. Halter (to prevent hard hands on the horse's mouth)
2. Surcingle or saddle (preferably a light racing training saddle to start)
3. Set of long lines (preferably 30 feet in length)
4. Leather strap (to tie stirrup irons together underneath the belly and resting at the length of the rider's leg)
5. Gloves to protect your hands

Horses who would benefit from long-lining

- Young horses being started under saddle
- Those being trained for carriages, sleighs, and buggies
- Performance horses in training and conditioning
- Equines in rehabilitation
- Those being brought back into work from an extended rest
- Geriatric horses who can no longer be under saddle, yet who would benefit from the attention, connection, and exercise
- Horses with issues such as biting, bolting, bucking, rearing and balking, and those lacking attention, motivation, or a spark in the eye
- Those who enjoy and appreciate variety and connection!

28

BE A TEAM LEADER

THERE IS NOTHING SO STRONG AS TRUE GENTLENESS AND NOTHING SO GENTLE AS QUIET STRENGTH.

I don't believe there is such a thing as a "bad" horse, but dangerous horses can quickly be created when they are misunderstood or mishandled.

Mishandling can take on many different forms, including force and abuse and lack of experience in identifying correct boundaries and behavior patterns.

My expectations are clear: "You don't hurt me and I don't hurt you, and together we can realize your full potential!"

Training pushy, playful horses to be respectful of bound-aries can be a challenge. Here's how to take on the task.

He was exquisite, a true specimen of majesty and beauty. I watched as the three-year-old black Friesian stallion quickly paced back and forth in the tiny stall he had to call home. With testosterone and energy coursing through his body, he barely knew what to do with himself. He was clearly uncomfortable cooped up in his small pen and I wondered how often he was able to spend time outside playing, exercising, and just being a horse.

This amazing fellow was being trained for a judging event called Keuring. But with an inexperienced guardian and a young trainer, things weren't going quite as planned. I was called in to assist because the barn staff was very concerned about the safety of both horse and humans, and I could see why. My visit was short, as I had flown in from out of state to consult. With just an hour to assess, advise, and potentially "fix" this predicament, I knew I had my work cut out for me.

I don't believe there is such a thing as a "bad" horse, but dangerous horses can quickly be created when they are misunderstood or mishandled. Mishandling can take on many different forms, including force and abuse and lack of experience in identifying correct boundaries and behavior patterns.

But a responsible trainer always remembers that no matter how good the horse is, if the client isn't on the same page, she can easily undo all the work that was done.

It is important to make sure that the horse owner or trainer can carry on your work and not confuse the horse with inconsistent or contradictory training and communication, and to teach the guardian the lessons she needs to carry this success into the future.

Who is Leading Who?

As with most of my consultations, I asked for the guardian to handle the horse so I could observe their interactions. My client began to enter the stall, but quickly came back out, as she wasn't comfortable in her horse's presence. Overexcited and unpredictable, he was simply too much for her to handle.

I then asked the trainer to lead the stallion to the arena so I would have a chance to observe the training. The stallion crowded the doorway. The trainer smacked the horse in the face to ask him to back up, placed the halter on and then led him comfortably to the arena, where she handed him over to the guardian.

The horse immediately engaged in a full battery of ornery and mischievous behavior. He was pulling my client in every direction, swinging his head, almost knocking her over, nibbling on her, and trying to take a chunk out of her side. With this entire happening, there was no chance for the guardian to lead him around the arena. Instead, she spent her time trying to avoid being stepped on, body slammed, and bitten. Her attention was on staying safely out of her horse's way and not giving him clear direction as the leader of her herd of two. It was abundantly clear who was leading whom.

The Change Comes From You

I asked the stallion's guardian why she was having trouble, and she told me she didn't want to offend him by schooling him. But her concern over not offending him had overshadowed her own safety and ability to be a true leader.

Next, I began working with the stallion. Through reading his facial features, energy, and body language, it was apparent after only a short time that this young horse wasn't malicious. He had simply learned to be disrespectful. His eye remained soft, his top lip extended in a mischievous manner, and the rest of his body and energy were playful, not aggressive. But this playfulness could change in a heartbeat and was only a thought away! We discussed the use of the Dually, a pressure halter I endorse and utilize in my practice. We switched halters, which in itself was quite the task. It was like trying to halter a piranha!

From my confident approach, the stallion knew this experience would be very different and immediately took a step back. It only took a few minutes to teach him to stand at attention, create space, and remain attentive, polite, and respectful. In fact, he was so good that I was taken aback by this instant transformation.

My expectations were clear: "You don't hurt me and I don't hurt you, and together we can realize your full potential!"

We made great progress as he proudly displayed his knowledge of "ground tying." Next, we moved into leading around the full arena with length in the line, right down to the mirror that had previously scared him at both a walk and trot in-hand. In just a single one-hour session, he was an entirely different horse.

Creating a Team

But a responsible trainer always remembers that no matter how good the horse is, if the client isn't on the same page she can easily undo all the work that was done. It is important to make sure that the horse owner or trainer can carry on your work and not confuse the horse with inconsistent or contradictory training and communication, and to teach the guardian the lessons she needs to carry this success into the future.

As I watched my client learn from observation, and then later with personal guidance, I was proud to see a team developing right before my eyes. All it took was just a few corrections for both parties to understand acceptable and unacceptable behavior and for everyone to remain safe and enjoy each other's company.

We started the day with a victim hunted by her horse, and ended with a partnership and winning team!

7 Safety Tips

1. Create the right environment for you and your horse to be safe and comfortable. Begin leading in a round pen or arena for safety, making sure you have proper footing, boundaries, and stimulus.

2. Wear the proper clothing, including paddock boots for foot protection, gloves to avoid rope burns, and a helmet if the horse has a tendency to strike and rear.

3. Have the right equipment with you (for example, a Dually halter, used correctly, and a 14-foot lead rope).

4. Approach with authenticity, making sure your body, mind, and communication are all in alignment.

5. Be completely present. Do not think about what has happened in the past or what could happen in the future.

6. Read your horse's intention. Capture the whisper in his eye or nose position.

7. Act with integrity, mutual respect and understanding.

Be sure to walk like a leader and have a true purpose. If there is a leadership void, your horse will fill it.

---

7 Training Tips

1. Never hit your horse, as this will encourage inappropriate behavior or confuse him. It can sometimes even be mistaken for petting and stroking, and can create head shyness. Simply correct his head carriage by moving his head away from you with your hand on the lead rope.

2. Your horse always follows his nose. Correct his nose carriage in the direction he needs to carry his head and body.

3. If you allow your horse to pull on the rope, he is leading you. This is mostly seen when handlers lead from the shoulder; instead, place the horse's

nose at your shoulder. Create a mutually acceptable placement where the lead rope is loose and you can walk together casually.

4. Horses learn from the release of pressure, not the pressure itself. Place your horse in the correct position by either backing him up to your shoulder or moving him forward to your shoulder, and then instantly release to create peace and quiet.

5. Who is moving whose feet? Be sure to walk like a leader and have a true purpose. If there is a leadership void, your horse will fill it.

6. Your horse's primary survival trait is awareness! Be sure to know what is happening around you so you can respond and not react.

7. Backing your horse up is a great way to create space, boundaries and trust. When your horse is unruly ask him to move his feet . . . backward!

Why You Might Have Trouble Leading Your Horse

- *Environment:* Insufficient space to roam, romp, and play.

- *Nutrition*: Excessive sweet feed/protein.

- *Lack of socialization:* A need for mutual grooming and interaction as well as behavioral guidelines and schooling.

- *Personal match:* "Green and green makes black and blue." Education is key.

- Ground manners: Require spook-busting and guidelines (DVD No. 6 of the *Reach Out to Natural Horsemanship Series, TLC* – Trust-Based Leadership and Compassionate Communication, is an ideal companion guide to leading).

- *Green horses:* Lack of exposure and handling.

- *Testosterone:* A horse is a horse is a horse, although leading stallions requires specific skills!

29

NATURE VS. NURTURE

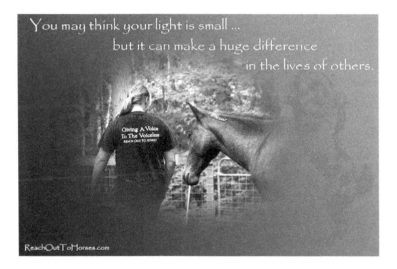

You may think your light is small ...
but it can make a huge difference
in the lives of others.

Giving A Voice
To The Voiceless
REACH OUT TO HORSES

ReachOutToHorses.com

I am often asked to help people with the horse they just can't handle. They've tried everything and their horse just will not stop its behavior; and, in some cases, drastic action will be taken if they or someone else can't "fix" the problem. To begin addressing these issues, I always steer my clients toward the behavior of the wild horse. Horses have survived through history using instinct, adaptation, and an effective non-verbal language that goes well beyond the unspoken. When observing horses in a natural habitat, you will find them running, bucking, rearing, kicking, and biting one another out of play. You will witness their curious, gregarious nature, along with their social interaction. You will not see them stall-walking, weaving, or wind-sucking!

It is crucial to remember that, so often, these majestic creatures are taken out of their natural environment and placed in a completely unfamiliar world. We force them to go against their natural instincts and behavior patterns without giving it a second thought.

Take a moment to imagine yourself to be a free-roaming horse.

Horses' Natural Behavior	Human Demands	How to Support Your Horses
Used to roaming in natural habitat several miles a day	Stalled for health & safety; Confinement in a 12 x 12 stall, which can affect the following: • Conformation in foals and horses • Socialization disorders • Emotional and mental state • Vices and habits can develop • Nutritional requirements not met and Self-medication not possible • Shuts down curiosity and motivation as well as natural habituation • Restricted exercise for muscle maintenance and bone growth	Ideally horses appreciate living in the most natural environment possible: a. Understand that horses are naturally claustrophobic! b. Live on acreage with horses naturally c. Turn-out in the day or at night d. Turn-out for a few hours e. Least desirable: stall with a run or stall alone f. Monitor baseline and behavior changes
Trickle feeders who graze 16–18 hours a day	Scheduled feeds and restricted food access may encourage or develop: • Colic, ulcers, etc. • Vices: cribbing, windsucking and weaving • Habits: box walking • Food aggression • Boredom • Eating manes and tails • Nutritional deficiencies	Ideas of support: a. Natural grazing b. Free feed c. Diet plan (Muscle testing); free choice minerals and dynamite d. Paddock paradise (Pete Ramey) e. Consider pros and cons of schedule f. Slow feeders g. Trickle feeders as toys

Horses' Natural Behavior	Human Demands	How to Support Your Horses
Feet as a primary and valuable tool of defense	*Asked to:* • *Pick up feet and pick out (even when tied)* • *Farrier support* • *Shoes are applied* • *When lacking compliance, a running W is introduced—feet are taken from underneath him* • *Chained to raise feet higher* • *Hobbled incorrectly* • *Legs are pin fired*	*Realize picking up your horse's feet is taking his primary form of defense from him.* *a. Gain trust: be mindful of who your horse trusts* *b. Gain respect and leadership (no leaning, pulling feet away)* *c. Prepare your horse to pick up his feet and gain complete balance* *d. Support him in preparation for the farrier—training is not the farrier's job* *e. Consider pain being an aspect of reluctance to pick up feet* *f. Know your horse's baseline to know what is normal and abnormal*
Herd animals and sociable individuals	*Expected to:* • *naturally interact with humans* • *Adapt to human demands* • *Stand in stalls with bars dividing from friends and family* • *Lack social interaction* • *Avoid mutual grooming* • *Not be involved with horse play* • *Abstain from recreational sex*	*Social interaction through:* *a. Natural environment* *b. Turn-out* *c. Removal of bars, walls, and fences—touching noses* *d. Match your horses with their pals for safety, partnership, and fun* *e. Be mindful of paddock and stall changes, departures, and deaths* *f. Playdates*
Natural flight instincts	*You have learned to:* • *Protect yourself through flight* • *Flight, fight, freeze phenomenon* • *Into-pressure phenomenon*	*Train your horse to go against his nature, to be able to:* *a. Handle pressure and come off pressure* *b. Accept stimulus* *c. Be prepared for unknown and unusual circumstances*

Horses' Natural Behavior	Human Demands	How to Support Your Horses
	All that goes against your nature: • Haltering • Leading • Loading • Tying • Clipping • Picking up feet • Flooding—a form of desensitizing	Be mindful of: d. Flight paths and flight options e. Understand behavior patterns f. Consider pain g. Capture the whisper What are you reprimanding for?
Blind areas—there are five predominant blind areas on horses (above their poll and back, below their nose and belly, up to 6 feet in front of them and directly behind them, 2 inches either side)	What we do to go against their nature: • Stroke the horse on on the forehead— third eye without consent • Approach directly from the front • First time saddling • Ride—sit in the blind area! • Apply pressure with our legs—blind and into pressure zone • Dressage, jumping, and showing—straight lines from memory	a. Approach in a paasive manner b. Approach with a soft angle c. Offer the back of the hand as an introduction; wait for permission to stroke between the eyes d. Prepare for the saddling process e. Appreciate the trust involved when riding f. Understand all horsemanship goes against the natural of horses
Equus – the silent language of the horse	People approach: • With great speed and lack of personal awareness • In the past and the future, but rarely in the present time • Loudly with predominantly verbal cues • Lacking knowledge in equine herd dynamics or behavior • Unaware how to capture the slightest gesture • Expecting an understanding of voice commands • Inauthentic	Learn: a. Understand herd dynamics and behavior b. Explore energy and energy healing c. Explore capturing the whisper through understanding minor body language gestures d. Study telepathy/ animal communication e. Teach your horse voice commands over time f. Practice being in the present time g. What is being authentic?

Horses' Natural Behavior	Human Demands	How to Support Your Horses
	Bonus:	
Health and well-being	Nature's elements take their toll	Come to understand the nature of the horse and create an ideal rearing program, ideal life
Many horses in the wild are known to live to their teens and early twenties vs 30s and 40s in captivity!	Heal through movement, rest, self-medication, rolling, etc.	
		Style, as well as a
	Awareness is part of leadership...	training program
		Introduce complimentary therapies to support your horse as an athlete (chiropractic, massage, acupressure, acupuncture, Reiki energy healing, therapeutic oils)
		`Be aware of your environment and your horse's responses—allow your horse to watch, listen, and learn

These are but a few changes we make to horses' daily lives and a few expectations we place on them. *Horses' instincts have been honed over the 54 million years that they have inhabited this planet and the relatively short period of time they have lived in domestication is certainly not enough to change the natural behaviors and instincts that have served them for so long.*

Many times, in fact, these natural behaviors can be seen in the "problems" of domesticated horses. Cribbing, for example, can be classed as a form of grazing. A cribbing horse may be lacking jaw movement and exercise, and because of that may start to chew other parts of his surroundings. The horse that "stall walks" or "weaves" is exercising his natural instinct to steadily forage. Understanding the natural behaviors and survival instincts will help you to better approach your horse's "problems" and "vices."

As horse trainers, riders, managers, and horse lovers, it is always our responsibility to investigate all possibilities. If you are working with someone else's horse, it is obviously useful to know the history from the owners. But you should then place that information in the back of your mind! It is far more important to read what the horse is telling you about his history. People perceive events in different ways, both from other people and especially from horses.

Although the history of the horse may explain some of the behaviors you observe, it is only the horse himself who can tell you the true story.

30

HORSE TALK IN THE SHOW RING

Never miss the magic of a moment! Don't forget to just BE

ReachOuttoHorses.com

When you watch the wild herds, only seldom do you hear their calls, as this would alert predators of their whereabouts. The odd whinny and rolling nicker can certainly be identified, but overall, the herds live in harmonious stillness together.

Horses talk in whispers. Generally speaking, this means they communicate through the slightest cue and gesture with one another and with us. It's a learned language best shown to them by their herd members and elders. When you watch the wild herds, only seldom do you hear their calls, as this would alert predators of their whereabouts. The odd whinny and rolling nicker can certainly be identified, but overall, the herds live in harmonious stillness together.

Once taken out of their natural habitat, wild horses will often be seen nestled together for security, simply startled to hear another horse call, initially confused by this act, as it brings attention to a vulnerable herd. It takes time for them to settle into their new home and realize that they are not being stalked. Their domestic counterparts will not have lived this natural lifestyle, and come from quite another perspective being rather comfortable to express themselves vocally. In fact, it is a compliment and quite moving when wild horses or mustangs whinny in your presence for the very first time, showing their trust in their home and in you.

However much horses' senses and communication have been dulled in domestication, they remain herd animals and revert back to natural tendencies, which can easily be identified in high-stress situations. A horse who finds himself out of his comfort zone will often call out to his own kind, be it to seek comfort, a response, or, indeed, to give a simple shout-out as a "hello." It's quite possible for a horse to identify a long-lost friend through his whinny and greet another from across the arena, the pasture, or car park, thus being quite the social butterfly. But come time for a show, whinnying and other vocalizations can be downright unhelpful as we ask our horses to be focused on us during this time.

Don't expect your horse to accept all stimuli at the showground naturally, for horses are flight animals and if they cannot get away they begin to fight, which is shown as "acting out."

There are several support systems we can put into place to create a positive off-site and showing experience.

Consider your horse's life experience because any new experience takes time to prepare and lead up to. Some horses take all that you present in their stride naturally, while others require some nurturing.

Before:

- Don't leave it until the day of the show to take your horse out on a date for the very first time and expect perfect performance.

- Do take the time that is needed to prepare your horse fully for what is yet to come. Many of my clients will take young horses on adventures in preparation for the big event; it may be a journey with a seasoned horse or simply a journey to the show grounds for a short visit and return home.

- Don't expect your horse to accept all stimuli at the showground naturally, for horses are flight animals and if they cannot get away they begin to fight, which is shown as "acting out."

- Do desensitize your horse to a variety of objects, items, and scenarios prior to the show. Gradually increase their tolerance level, all the while releasing pressure to praise their tries.

- Don't practice purely in the comfort of your own home/arena and believe it will translate to all new situations.

- Do practice in multiple locations, as horses are associative thinkers. They see in pictures and will associate the exact location with the act you performed. They need opportunities for this to extend to new locations and in order to feel comfortable with the new environment.

Horses are sensitive to energy. They feel your agenda, intentions, and emotions while you are handling them on the ground and while you ride.

Frustration is a sign of lack of patience, understanding, and creativity. Who you are when the situation is challenging shows who you are as a person.

During:

- Don't arrive at the show under time constraints, thus creating pressure on yourself and your horse(s). Horses are sensitive to energy. They feel your agenda, intentions, and emotions while you are handling them on the ground and while you ride.

- Instead, give yourself plenty of time to settle in, prepare yourself and your horse physically, mentally, and emotionally. Consider ways to remove all kinds of pressure.

- Don't simply saddle up and go into the warm-up or show ring!

- Instead, consider how long your horse needs to settle in. Would it be over a night, a day, or a morning? Does your horse appreciate being shown around the facility as you walk around and familiarize yourself with a new location? Take the time that is needed to listen to your horse's needs. Provide the comforts of home away from home.

- Don't become a dominant rider, allowing your frustration to come through. Be it toward yourself or your horse, your horse feels the tension and believes it's toward him. Frustration is a sign of lack of patience, understanding, and creativity. Who you are when the situation is challenging shows who you are as a person. When life gives you lemons, it's time to create lemonade.

- Instead, recognize your and your horse's strengths and weaknesses and be prepared to be the leader your horse wants you to be. Understand his/her needs and provide them with the inner strength and awareness of a true leader. Step up and recognize what your horse needs from you in that moment, acknowledge their needs and provide the right resolution. After all, it's not about you, it's about the team success!

Afterward:

- Reflect upon the joint experience. Ask yourself:
  o What could we have done differently or improved upon?
  o What were our strengths, best moments, and successes?
  o How can we make it even better next time?

- Praise your horse anyway—understand he has given you his best effort for that particular moment and that particular day, as you have too.

- *Celebrate!*

When we come to realize that everything our horses do is done for a reason, despite the fact we may not understand or recognize exactly what they are, all becomes easier.

The art of horsemanship includes having a plan and not falling in love with it.

Perfect planning and training certainly prepare horse and rider for a positive experience, but flexibility and open-mindedness continue to play an important role.

Give yourself and your horse the space to have fun and succeed! Remember the very reason you entered the world of horses….

My Spanish Mustang, Excalibur, once accompanied me to the Rocky Mountain Horse Expo to demonstrate the Reach Out to Horses methodologies during a "Saddle-up and Spook-bust" demonstration while being the ambassador for the Spanish Mustang. Naturally, he was the star of the show! With a solid, trust-based partnership, he raised the roof. There had been no specific preparation leading up to this event. In fact, due to my touring schedule, Excalibur spent most of the year at our home ranch with his herd. The weather didn't permit us to practice prior to the demonstration, except for three rides the week leading up to the event. Time was spent to explain to him that we would be demonstrating to hundreds of people, and knowing his character meant that I knew he loved to perform—spontaneously. His needs were met and we did just that!

Something to "Chew" On

Horses make many communicative gestures with their mouths. They will begin to lick and chew, sometimes opening their mouths, while at other times keeping the jaw closed. This gesture shows that they are relaxed. It also means that they are herbivores and if they are in a place to eat, they feel safe and we are not doing any harm.

You may have observed this gesture when young horses make this motion out of respect for their elders—known as clacking or snapping. It's a sign of submission. It's also a sign that your horse is digesting and understanding information that he has been faced with.

31

RESTARTING RESCUES AND REHABS UNDER SADDLE

OPINION IS THE LOWEST FORM OF KNOWLEDGE. IT REQUIRES NO ACCOUNTABILITY, NO UNDERSTANDING. THE HIGHEST FORM OF KNOWLEDGE IS EMPATHY, FOR IT REQUIRES US TO SUSPEND OUR EGOS AND LIVE IN ANOTHER'S WORLD. IT REQUIRES PROFOUND PURPOSE LARGER THAN THE SELF.

REACHOUTTOHORSES.COM

Teaming up with rescues to support both horses and their stewards is part of our mission statement at Reach Out to Horses.

There was a time in my life when I introduced hundreds of horses to their first saddle, bridle, and rider in thirty minutes during workshops and demonstrations. Through gentling untouched horses from all walks of life, including wild mustangs, Premarin mares, and feral tribal horses, I learned to adapt and truly hone my skills of horse whispering to capture the whisper and listen to their individual needs.

Teaming up with rescues to support both horses and their stewards is part of our mission statement at Reach Out to Horses. No matter the horse's breed, age, disposition, conformation, or background, we do not discriminate.

To prepare horses for their lives as athletes and future careers, it's common to start them under saddle between the ages of two and four years. Naturally, there is an ideal age, which depends entirely on their physical, mental, and emotional needs. No one horse is the same as another, and yet it can be that their destiny took another direction to bring them to this very point later in life.

It has been said that older horses are more challenging to start under saddle and that "you cannot teach an old horse new tricks." Although I have not found that particular statement to hold merit, I do believe that there can be unique challenges surrounding a fully developed athletic horse or an individual who is set in their ways. The younger mind and body can often be shaped and developed with greater ease.

If you find yourself blessed to invite a wise soul into your life, or if you are giving them another chance for a future of their choice, ask yourself how you can best serve their needs. It's imperative to seek professional advice and ensure that each horse is ready for this life adjustment before embarking on any training path:

Through clear observation, your horse will show you his physical, emotional, and mental scars, as well as the experiences and accolades he has gathered.

Consider your horse's immediate needs:

- Veterinary examination: health check and physical support

- Nutritional support: detox, correct diet, weight gain or loss

- Farrier: removal of shoes, corrective shoeing, trims

- Dentistry: annual check-ups

- Deworming: fecal samples prior to chemical or natural deworming

- Chiropractic adjustments and other complementary therapies: maintain physical health and wellbeing

- Respite: following a rough career or life situation

Professional advice is not the only piece you need to ensure a mutually successful time together. It's important that you take your whole horse into account.

Horse's History:

Often, we want to know all that we can about our horse's history. Through clear observation, your horse will show you his physical, emotional, and mental scars, as well as the experiences and accolades he has gathered. Have an open heart and mind to see all that is possible and allow your horses to blossom and share supporting them to find their true potential (once again).

Past Traumas:

There is an art to protecting our horses and yet (at the same time) not surrounding them with bubble wrap. Honor your horses for who they are today and allow them to reveal their history. Realize that their memories stay with them for life; they may cover them up and hide them deeply or allow us to see them in time. Often, these kinds of memories show themselves through inappropriate behavior, stable vices, and habits or tendencies such as learned helplessness and disassociation. Give your horse the space he needs and offer a place of healing and support.

Physical limitations:

Age brings with it life's experiences as well as some marks, scars, and bruising. Horses are often discarded because they didn't fit the ideal that another had put on them. Although conformation cannot be changed, posture can. Although not every horse is physically sound, neither is every human. When we accept our horses in sickness and in health, for richer and poorer, our lives become fuller. You may need to be mindful of any physical limitations and how this may affect their training and future career under saddle. You may even need to go slow in the training and become more creative and be flexible with your plan.

When we accept our horses in sickness and in health, for richer and poorer, our lives become fuller.

Environment:

There is much to be said about the correct environment. Horses in nature are happy, generally healthy and whole. The more we can imitate a natural environment the better it is for our horses. Now extend this mentality into the workplace and include the appropriate facility, training strategy, and trainer. Gauge the success of your choices by how smoothly your relationship moves forward.

Emotional and mental state:

Often an overlooked part of horsemanship and yet an essential component to truly embrace your whole horse. You may have to allow considerable time for your horse to be able to begin a new lifestyle. Time-off in nature is a wonderful cure and is often just what the vet ordered. If your horse seems vacant, take the time that is needed to allow him to find himself. Once the spark is back in the eye you know he is feeling better! Look for the connection and appreciate all tries.

Time of trust:

Take the time to take the time. Truly! Build trust at home and in all situations. Trust is earned and not given. When you see what your horse needs from you and you, in turn, provide it, the gift of trust will be bestowed. Do not force your horse or place dominance over him; this is not the way of a true leader!

Your imprint!

Realize this is the imprint you make on your horse, just like parents make on a child. I believe that the day we start a horse under saddle for the very first time is one of the most important days of its life. This day can be marked as one of the most magical experiences or, in contrast, a very traumatic time. It's the trainer's responsibility to ensure the horse remembers this day favorably—today, you are the trainer!

The fundamentals of inviting an older horse to give you permission to ride within a trust-based partnership are no different than having raised a foal into adulthood. For a healthy being, both require a human with core values and the ability to provide a safe home. Although we cannot guarantee what the future holds, we can hold a place in our hearts and homes for our horses to feel that they have come "home." It's with mutual respect and understanding that we begin to learn how to reach out and touch each horse individually. As you give your gifts, they will be returned immeasurably.

32

HANDLING COMMON HERD DYNAMICS

ReachOuttoHorses.com

Good Fences Make Good Neighbors
~ Robert Frost

Without the wisdom of their elders, the young are at a severe disadvantage as they venture into unchartered dominant territory.

Put a group of horses together and you will witness herd dynamics unfold before your eyes. Within moments, the dance of establishing leadership and other roles within the herd will begin. The horses will become extremely "vocal," and will establish rank through challenging behavior that can be as subtle as a glance or an ear movement, or as bold as moving the other horses' feet, charging, biting, kicking, and squealing.

218 | Beyond the Barn

The Natural Herd

Under more natural conditions, individual horses adopt very specific roles to secure a safe and harmonious herd environment. Some horses can be born into leadership positions, groomed by their parents over time to become all that they can be. These "heirs apparent" usually display a more passive form of leadership, while other horses fight their way to the top, bringing forth a dominant style of leadership. A common misconception is that the alpha mare rules. The dominant mare is commonly the second in command, ensuring much of the leadership when forced into interaction. As we find both loners and socialites among people, we find them in the horse world too. Those seeking adventure balance out those seeking a simple life. There are natural-born leaders and natural-born followers.

Forced Herd Dynamics

Under unnatural circumstances, however, these healthy relationships can go awry. This often happens in our attempts to develop small herds of horses in pastures and paddocks, either at home or in boarding barn situations.

Think about a classroom of juveniles ruling themselves, or of adolescents without parental guidance—where would this lead? It would lead to the very same place it takes foals who find themselves orphaned, or yearlings allowed to frolic without supervision: a misguided place that often causes future behavioral challenges or social ineptitude. Without the wisdom of their elders, the young are at a severe disadvantage as they venture into unchartered dominant territory. Often, the leader is not the most aggressive horse, but instead leads by strong example, by simply "being," observing all, and acting only when needed. While wild horses will gather cordially during daily waterhole rituals, isolated non-socialized stallions may have a propensity for extreme violence and even potentially life-threatening injury.

Understanding Disruptive Herd Behavior

It would be remiss to overlook our horses' environment as a reason for possible disruptions in herd behavior, since space is a distance concern for these animals. Behavior is often accentuated in small enclosures, and often sees this in situations where horses are confined to smaller paddocks and pastures. Space is crucially important for your horse's health and well-being; it gives horses an opportunity to get away from one another, or from the herd, if necessary. This helps prevent negative interactions and injuries. The ability to move around freely is a must!

Another obvious behavior influencer for domesticated horses is the introduction or removal of food. Horses are natural-born grazers and are used to being surrounded by an abundance of food. Fighting often occurs when there is a lack of food. Remove the lack of food (by providing adequate pasture or hay) and harmony is reintroduced to the herd. If you don't have the means to create the ideal feeding scenario, slow feeders are essential.

Adjusting Habits and Patterns for a Happy Herd

If you and your horses are happy and healthy, then keep up the good work. If it isn't broken, then don't fix it! However, if you are concerned with the dynamics of the herd or your horses have incurred physical injuries, it may be time to consider making some changes and reviewing your horse-keeping methods and circumstances. Take time to review your habits and patterns to find an all-around better solution.

If your horse:

- **Has been moved recently:** Try accommodating for this time of transition and be the support he needs during this adjustment period.

- **Is not accepted in the herd:** Evaluate his personality, role, and past and current mental, emotional, and physical health. Try building him up (through physical and complementary therapies and nutritional support).

- **Is crowding the gate:** Try training him to take a step back and create a safe entrance space or organize feeders from the outside of the paddocks for your own safety.

- **Has a sudden behavior change:** Try reviewing all recent changes to determine the cause and have him checked physically.

- **Does not want to be caught:** Try to discover the true cause of this behavior, be it pain-related, ill-fitting tack, your relationship, his activities/discipline, or simply a lack of motivation and energy or his strong desire to be with his family herd.

- **Is classed as herd-bound:** Try building a stronger partnership through a trust-based connection while discovering his motivation.

While we certainly do our best to develop herd situations that will work well for our domesticated horses, it can be a challenging feat at times. Each horse is an individual and things can constantly shift and change with each horse and the herd as a whole. Provide your horses with as much pasture space and food resources as possible to help prevent disagreements and injuries. With a little understanding and observation, you will be able to help create the best possible herd situation for your horses.

The Effects of Poor Training or Socialization on Herd Behavior

- Over-handling foals can result in crowding and unsuitable behavior/habits.

- Lack of socialization can develop into social ineptness.

- Lack of knowledge and boundaries can show up as a horse crossing boundaries and displaying aggressive tendencies with his herd mates.

- Incorrect hand feeding can create crowding, mugging, and biting behaviors.

- The stall-bound horse will have pent-up energy, vices/habits, physical issues, lack of socialization, and possible dangerous behaviors.

- Horses kept in a stressful environment display vices/habits and emotional, mental, and physical issues.

- Horses that have experienced fear-based training show displacement/depression and aggressive tendencies.

Under Pressure

- Horses will raise their heads or plant their feet when they feel pressure on their poll for the first time.

- Young horses will expand their stomachs and breathe into the girth or into the rider's legs when they feel pressure against their side.

- The first time they feel the bit pressure on the left side of their mouths, horses will try to turn right—into the sensation and pressure.

- Horses will often slow down when they feel a whip on their sides.

Developed over millions of years, this behavior is part of a horse's survival instinct. They have to be shown how they can release themselves from this same pressure. The key is in the timing of the release.

This same phenomenon becomes apparent when you place incorrect pressure behind a horse you are trying to load through lines, whip, and people shouting. Your horse will immediately run backward out of the trailer and into the pressure.

33

TEACHING YOUR HORSE TO TIE

One key to training your horse to tie well is teaching him to yield to pressure in situations that are stress-free before introducing him to stressful scenarios.

Another key to successfully training your horse to tie is to address the emotional and mental factors that create a "non-tying horse" to begin with.

There are many situations in which it's important for your horse to tie well. It could be for the vet or farrier, at a show or event, or perhaps while you are grooming and tacking up. While it may seem simple enough, your horse may have quite a different perspective.

As prey animals, horses have a strong inborn desire to flee in the face of perceived danger. When a horse is tied he can't respond in this way. For the uninitiated or fearful horse, this can set off alarm bells and send him into a state of frantic panic, particularly if there is no breaking point or release in sight.

It is also important to recognize that horses are innately "into pressure" beings and, by their very nature. they lean into the point of pressure. This leads a horse to lean into you when you press on his flank, rump, or other part of his body; or to raise his head high when asked to follow the feel of the lead rope.

Without any support or formal trust-based training, it is unlikely that a horse will automatically take to being tied. While some horses may learn fairly easily to accept being tied, others may have had experiences where they've broken their halters, hitching posts, or worse, and have subsequently developed a phobia to tying. The good news is that no matter what his age, any horse can be taught what is expected of him if you use a kind and patient manner.

Set your horse up for success

There are number of things you can teach and practice with your horse to help prepare him for being able to tie well. By taking the time to do this work and approaching the task in an open, empathetic and supportive manner, you can create powerful and lasting results while avoiding mistakes or gaps in training that will require fixing later.

Pressure and Release

One key to training your horse to tie well is teaching him to yield to pressure in situations that are stress-free before introducing him to stressful scenarios. The first rule is to never attempt to tie without first exploring your horse's knowledge of pressure and release.

Some simple yet essential exercises to prepare for tying include:

- Neck stretches and yields following the feel of the line
- Light-touch head drops
- Forward and back rocking horse steps
- Altering gait and speed while leading

As the exercises build on one another, make sure to create times for your horse to feel somewhat restricted while being given a chance to find a way out using collaborative communication.

Desensitization Exercises

Once your horse fully understands how to get himself out of trouble by coming forward toward the pressure, it is time to introduce him to some surprises. It's easy to teach him to tie when everything is calm, but you would be remiss if you didn't prepare him for the unexpected and provide him with appropriate coping skills for those stressful or startling moments.

Before tying a horse anywhere, integrate some in-hand, spook-busting methods:

- Desensitize to scary objects and items
- Desensitize to startling and unusual sounds
- Graduate to an in-hand obstacle course of higher learning

Building Confidence

Another key to successfully training your horse to tie is to address the emotional and mental factors that create a "non-tying horse" to begin with. Training is essential to building the horse's confidence in both himself and in you and will allow you to create a trust-based partnership.

This can be done over time as your horse learns to come into himself more, leave the herd behind, explore and venture off campus, and experience a multitude of environments and situations. Once he has a good foundation of confidence, you can gradually introduce him to new locations and scenarios, and increase the stimuli that will trigger fears, such as a fear of isolation. Soon, fear will be replaced with the understanding that he is safe, even when you are asking him to be restricted or isolated for a time.

Training Your Horse to Tie

The simplest way to begin is to loop the line over a hitching post to create some resistance, and hold it in your hand while grooming! This way, the horse does not hit a rigid line and panic, which could put both of you at risk of bodily harm. Instead, your horse will be able to feel the give while at the same time making a pleasant association with tying through mindful grooming.

This same looping method applies while teaching the horse to tie at a trailer, wash rack, or other location, keeping in mind the necessity for excellent footing and surrounding safety. Naturally, the horse finds himself in a pressure/release situation and you may decide to include food as a reward to enhance the situation while expediting the lesson.

You may also want to introduce the quick-release knot, popular around the world. It gives a similar sense of resistance but still gives you a chance to release the horse should he panic.

Some equestrians swear by the tradition of tying to a piece of string or bailing twine on a tie ring to ensure breakaway. Although some believe that horses can learn their own strength by snapping these strings, and that you should never allow them to breakaway, I have seen it save lives. While this tradition remains prevalent, its popularity is being overridden by the blocker tie ring, which provides soft resistance and safe tying without using knots.

If all else fails and your horse is truly phobic, you may decide to ground-tie him by simply teaching him to stand still when the attached lead rope is placed on the ground close by. It's a pretty easy "trick" to start with and moves effortlessly into all you do when you ask your horse to stand!

Remember that teaching your horse to tie goes beyond simply seeking a place for him to stand and wait—it is an introduction to the concepts of patience, respect, focus, and a time to process.

Work With, Not Against, Your Horse

From decades of experience worldwide, I have witnessed many approaches and seen some horrendous tying styles, ranging from snubbing posts to solitary standing stalls. Although it is customary for trainers to state that their methods work, these harmful and sometimes even cruel training styles simply aren't necessary and reflect a fear-based, dominance style of training.

Remember that teaching your horse to tie goes beyond simply seeking a place for him to stand and wait—it is an introduction to the concepts of patience, respect, focus, and a time to process.

The bottom line is to recognize that tying is not something that comes "naturally" to a horse. Choosing a style of training that supports and works with your horse's mind and encourages trust, not dominance, will help him find success with being tied and will create fewer issues down the road.

34

FOCUSING ON THE FEET

Tell me and I forget.
Teach me and I remember.
Involve me and I learn.

ReachOuttoHorses.com

It is never the farrier's job to train our horses for trimming.

This seems like common sense but it can easily be forgotten until the moment the farrier shows up. It is our responsibility as guardians to make sure our horses are suitably prepared. As highly trained and talented as your farrier might be, he is not a trainer, and the way he may choose to deal with a misbehaving horse may not be what you had in mind or fit into your training philosophy.

If you begin working with your horse at a young age and teach him manners and protocol, he will be ready by the time he needs to meet the farrier. Sounds easy, but it takes a lot of preparation and patience!

If you are looking to create and nurture a trust-based partnership with your horse, you have to learn to ask and not tell—acknowledge every "try," and remain compassionate in your communication.

> *You want a willing and relaxed participant,*
> *not one who is terrified and in pain.*

Practice makes Perfect

If you want to gently influence your horse's feet, create leverage, be more effective with less effort, help desensitize your horse to all lower extremity needs, and make working with his feet easy and enjoyable, a simple rope is your best tool (I like my ROTH Equine Education Rope).

Using the rope, practice:

- Moving your horse's leg in all directions, safely, while staying out of the kick zone and desensitizing your horse to the feeling of the rope all over and around his legs.

- Replacing instinctive fight-or-flight reactions with calm, relaxed responses.

- Educating your horse to yield to pressure, enhancing his understanding and willing participation.

This method is helpful for horses of all ages and experience levels—from foals and green or handled horses to those that require some retraining after a trauma or accident. With a little time and practice, your horse will become a star for leg and hoof handling. Best of all, it will keep you in your farrier's good books, and that is an important place to be!

35

NOT THE HOMECOMING
I HAD HOPED FOR

NO ONE EVER INJURED THEIR EYESIGHT BY LOOKING ON THE BRIGHT SIDE!

REACHOUTTOHORSES.COM

You Just Might Save Your Horses Life with Some of These Helpful Tips

I once arrived home after an amazing Healing Horses experience at Bitterroot Ranch in Wyoming, happy to be home and spend time with my herd. I ventured out on the ranch Monday morning and my equine soul mate, Excalibur, was already calling me. He immediately caught my attention with his rolling nicker and stance.

A bout of springtime laminitis had come calling, and I sprang into action.

Springtime is a good time to share some of the things you can do during a laminitis emergency while waiting for your vet to arrive.

Using some of these suggestions, you might just save your horse's life.

Check and/or integrate:

Gums for color, mucus, and capillary refill

Pulse in the hoof

Distorted hoof/rings

Hot hooves

High temp

Heart rate

Weight shifting

Shortened stride

Overweight

Diarrhea

We Applied:

Dynamite's Release spray

Dynamite's Dyna-pro for gut support

Dynamite's TNT, Excel, and OxMega

Cold hosed legs for 20 minutes

Applied Dynamite Miracle Clay to feet/legs

BEMER Blanket—for circulatory support

Young Living Essential Oils: Peppermint, Lemongrass, Release, and PanAway

Hands-on healing and long-distance Reiki

Foot support

New turnout in sand-based round pen

Meditation and visualization

Banamine

Farrier visit/check

A FULL RECOVERY

We treated Excalibur holistically, and nearly entirely naturally, only giving him Bute when it was absolutely necessary to control his pain. Now, several years later, Excalibur is out with his herd, grazing the pastures that are suitable for his dietary needs, with not too many sugary grasses to which he can have access. He regularly gallops with his girls and lives the life of a free horse once more!

Statements made on this page about Young Living Essential Oils, Dynamite Supplements and ROTH Protocol have not been evaluated by the FDA. These products and information are not intended to diagnose, treat, cure or prevent any disease. Anyone suffering from disease or injury should consult with a physician or veterinarian. If you or your animal are currently on medication, please DO NOT STOP.

ACKNOWLEDGMENTS

B y far, this has been the most challenging two decades of my life and at the same time the most rewarding road less traveled. The journey to follow the call of the horse has taken me beyond the barn and out into brand new "arenas," opportunities I could not have envisioned in my wildest dreams. I have been faced with some of my greatest challenges and been compensated with unexpected, unimaginable rewards.

First and foremost, I would like to thank all of the horses who have paved the way for me to learn to listen to their whispers and hear their gentle voice. It is through their wisdom that all of us who are blessed to be touched by them are expanding our consciousness and becoming better horsemen and women. Their patience is unparalleled as they seek only to be understood. There is nothing quite like looking into our horse's eye to witness the strength of the equine warrior.

Silently they wait as we take one step at a time to become the guardian they wish us to be while adventuring on our own personal crusade. Their language of movement is monumental in defining our ROTH methodologies, and as such the new paradigm of the next generation of natural horsemanship. The desire to pioneer these pathways comes from within and with it the trust, strength, and belief we can inspire change.

Not for lack of heart, desire and dedication my only sadness is that time and resources stand in the way of my reaching more lives. But I continue to try. It is my hope that this book reaches far and wide, and in doing so touches the lives of horses and their humans to effect further change and transform partnerships.

My gratitude is extended to all those who believed and continue to believe in me, displaying their trust through publishing our writings. It's because of you that this book came to life.

To Lacey Knight, Safia Khider, and Tess Helmandollar. Your small and yet steadfast team came together to capture the true essence of this book, tirelessly exploring two decades of writings to create our safely structured, solid and yet free-flowing approach, digestible for all to encapsulate. Through creative designs, hearts' desire to help all horses, and an unwavering belief in the mission your efforts supported me in bringing this vision forward.

To my husband, I owe all. He is my rock, my confidant, and my love. He chose to walk this path with me without knowing the magnitude of the commitment that lay before him. Unconditionally, he opens his heart to the horses and provides them with shelter and support. His talents surpass him, as he continues to explore all opportunities tirelessly forging the way through unchartered territory, adding his touch to all projects. Without his incredible desire and ability to learn all in life and his most meticulous means we would not be where we are today—as a team. Everyone needs a "Vin" and I am the lucky one to call you my husband. Thank you!

ABOUT
ANNA TWINNEY AND
REACH OUT TO HORSES

R each Out to Horses is the most comprehensive equine training program in the world with its foundations in communication, collaboration, and compassion. From the ground to the saddle, from the foal to the geriatric, and from the casual trail partner to the top dressage competitor, Reach Out to Horses (ROTH) teaches how to create a genuine partnership between horse and human, based in trust and clear communication not dominance. It is also the only program that teaches the true language of the horse, combining body language, animal communication, and the understanding and manipulation of energy.

Putting down the cookie-cutter approach to horsemanship, ROTH works with each horse as an individual, taking into account the horse's likes, dislikes, character, personality, learning style, abilities, preferences, and even hopes and dreams. This allows them to be a cocreator in their training and in their lives with humans.

The founder of Reach Out to Horses, Anna Twinney has traveled the world extensively, coaching this unique methodology to people from all walks of life and all equine disciplines. From all over the US and Europe, to Australia, Costa Rica, Morocco, China, and other countries, Anna has taught the ROTH philosophy on virtually every continent. 2018 marked the celebration of the twentieth year of her journey as an international horsewoman, clinician, equine behaviorist, linguist, teacher, coach, animal communicator, and Usui Holy Fire Reiki Master.

Anna's mission through her work with Reach Out to Horses, as an animal communicator and Usui Holy Fire Reiki Master, is to change the way the human world sees and works with their equine companions, as well as all of our planetary companions—to teach the world to capture the whisper and give a voice to the voiceless.